CONCILIUM

DIAKONIA
CHURCH FOR THE OTHERS

NORBERT GREINACHER and NORBERT METTE

CONCILIUM

Religion in the Eighties

CONCILIUM

General Secretariat: Prins Bernhardstraat 2, 6521 AB Nijmegen, The Netherlands

Concilium 198 (4/1988): Practical Theology

CONCILIUM

List of Members

Advisory Committee: Practical Theology

Directors:

Norbert Greinacher	Tübingen	West Germany
Norbert Mette	Münster	West Germany

Members:

Carlos Abaitua	Vitoria	Spain
Rosemary Crumlin RSM	Victoria	Australia
Virgil Elizondo	San Antonio, Texas	USA
Segundo Galilea	Santiago	Chile
Alfonso Gregory	Rio de Janeiro	Brazil
Frans Haarsma	Nijmegen	The Netherlands
Adrian Hastings	Harare	Zimbabwe
François Houtart	Louvain-la-Neuve	Belgium
Jan Kerkhofs	Louvain	Belgium
Hubert Lepargneur OP	São Paulo	Brazil
Anthony Lobo SJ	Washington, DC	USA
Angelo Macchi SJ	Milano	Italy
Alois Müller	Luzern	Switzerland
Thomas Nyiri	Budapest	Hungary
Emile Pin	Poughkeepsie, NY	USA
+Karl Rahner SJ	Innsbruck	Austria
Rosemary Ruether	Evanston, Ill.	USA
Heinz Schuster	Saarbrücken	West Germany
Sidbe Semporé	Cotonou	Benin
Francisco Soto	Jalapa, Veracruz	Mexico
Yorick Spiegel	Frankfurt, Main	West Germany
Wevitavidanelage, Don Sylvester	Colombo	Sri Lanka
Rolf Zerfass	Höchberg	West Germany

DIAKONIA: CHURCH FOR OTHERS

Edited by
Norbert Greinacher
and
Norbert Mette

English Language Editor
James Aitken Gardiner

T. & T. CLARK LTD
Edinburgh

August 1988
ISBN: 0 567 30078 1

ISSN: 0010-5236

Typeset by C. R. Barber & Partners (Highlands) Ltd, Fort William
Printed by Page Brothers (Norwich) Ltd

Concilium: Published February, April, June, August, October, December.
Subscriptions 1988: UK: £27.50 (including postage and packing); USA: US$49.95 (including air mail postage and packing); Canada: Canadian$59.95 (including air mail postage and packing); other countries: £27.50 (including postage and packing).

CONTENTS

Concilium 198 Special Column

The Seoul Olympics
  JOHN A. COLEMAN   xi

DIAKONIA:
CHURCH FOR OTHERS

Editorial
  NORBERT GREINACHER
  NORBERT METTE   xvii

Part I
Distress that calls to Heaven: Focus of Human Need

A Divided World. Can We Escape Mutual Injury and
Self-Destruction?
  ADEBAYO ADEDEJI   3

Victims in the Affluent Society
  GREGORY BAUM   14

Part II
'I see the Distress of my People':
Divine Compassion as a Christian Commission

Good News to the Poor
  CARLOS H. ABESAMIS   25

'Making Earth into Heaven': Diakonia in the Early Church
  NORBERT BROX   33

Church for Others
  OTTMAR FUCHS   41

The Prophetic Diakonia: The Church's Contribution to
Forming Humanity's Future
  FREI BETTO   55

Part III
Areas of Conflict in Diaconal Praxis

Diakonia in the Church of the Rich and the Church of the
Poor: A Comparative Study in Empirical Ecclesiology
  HERMANN STEINKAMP   65

Solidarity with the Lowliest: Parish Growth Through the
Witness of Practical Service
  NORBERT METTE   76

'Waiting at Table': A Critical Feminist Theological Reflection
on Diakonia
  ELISABETH SCHÜSSLER FIORENZA   84

Diakonia in Universal Context: An African Point of View
  PATRICK KALILOMBE   95

Diakonia as an Agency in the Welfare State
  JOHANNES DEGEN   102

Cultural Diakonia
  GOTTHARD FUCHS   110

Prospect

'But if you say so!' A Plea for a Church of the Diakonia
  ULRICH BACH   123

Contributors   132

CONCILIUM 198 Special Column

John A. Coleman

The Seoul Olympics

LET THE Olympic games begin! When the young French aristocrat, Pierre de Coubertin, proposed a revival of the ancient Olympic games he entertained plucky hopes that they would transcend politics and be a harbinger of world peace. Yet the first international games in Athens in 1896 whipped up so much chauvinistic jingoism among the Greeks that, within the year, they agitated toward a Cretan war against the Turks!

Coubertin's high ideal of trans-political Olympic games which would represent internationalism at its best, a celebration of the human body and spirit and a solemn acknowledgement of human commonalities, remains ever precarious. In Berlin in 1936 and Los Angeles in 1984 an unsporting and exaggerated host country's nationalism prevailed to soil the games. Ever since the Soviet Union joined the Olympics in 1952, a kind of mutual 'cold war in sports' has put its stamp on the games.

In Mexico, 1968, riot police fired randomly into a crowd to kill nearly 500 student demonstrators and in Munich, 1972, brute assassins made the innocent blood of Israeli athletes flow. Thus, since Montreal in 1976, the Olympic host city has become a species of armed camp to thwart the terrorists. Much of the West boycotted Moscow in 1980 and the Eastern bloc reciprocated in 1984. Indeed, in the early 1980s the very future of the international Olympic games was cast in doubt. So, the first unified games in over a decade in Seoul means that the ancient dream and hope remains alive. If the world can co-operate enough to stage the games, perhaps, the dream of creating something rather larger than the games is not entirely utopian.

The Olympic Motto

The motto of the Olympic games reads: altius, citius, fortius; *higher, faster, stronger. This motto spurs on the world's athletes to self-surpassing excellence. We spectators, too, thrill to see this stretch of human sinew and skill. It is time, however, for world opinion to insist that the International Olympic Committee (1) aim* higher *so that the Olympics become more a true symbol of international co-operation and a worthy celebration of athletic excellence; (2) move* faster *to remove the deformations in the Olympics; and (3) take* stronger *measures to curb the powers of the industrial-sports-media complex which, since Los Angeles and, again, at the winter games in Calgary last fall, has introduced a new crass commercialization into the Olympics.*

Aim Higher

Bruce Kidd, a former international track champion from Canada, has suggested that the Olympic games, as part of their opening and closing ceremonies, should contain a call by all the peoples of the world upon the superpowers to end the arms race and foster the international solidarities needed to solve world hunger, disease and poverty. We could take a wider advantage of this festival which convokes the whole world through sports to insert a narrow wedge to campaign for some other things which would keep us as a world together: a nurturing care for the environment, a more than 'merely' symbolic respect for the equality of nations, a deeper education about different cultures. Detente in one arena, such as sports, gives breathing space for a wider detente. At Los Angeles, a splendid international festival of arts accompanied the games. In Seoul, an academic convocation—largely under religious sponsorship—on the eve of the games will treat of mutual respect for cultural values in an interdependent world. These other events can counter-balance an over-politicized competitive spirit. Surely, the church which preaches an international common good and refuses to serve as an ideological vehicle for bloc formation cannot be indifferent to the true success of these games in Seoul.

Move Faster

The International Olympic Committee remains still too much an elitist and masculine (77 men, 3 women members) and first-world 'club'. It needs to be opened up more to the Eastern bloc and the Third World. Moreover, revenues from corporate advertising at the games should be more generously distributed to support athletics in the Third World. First world athletes enjoy heavy subsidy of their governments and private donors. A truly international sporting event will move to expand the financial base for equal chances for athletes from Zaire, Peru, Pakistan. Moreover, men's events outnumber women's sports two to one and media coverage of men's sports remains disproportionate. This needs monitoring by the I.O.C.

Take Stronger Measures

At the Los Angeles games, for the first time, the Olympics were presided over by a private corporation which undertook a special and aggressive campaign to obtain corporate and media advertisement and sponsorship. The Olympic stars were sold like breakfast food. The I.O.C., itself, has made peace with this new commercialization, indeed fostered it for Seoul. Commercial elites increasingly control crucial aspects of the Olympic movement. The Olympic committee needs to say to corporate and media sponsors: You will not be allowed to telecast our games and reach this world audience for your product unless you do so in ways in which the Olympic ideal of solidarity in sports is truly enhanced. The I.O.C. can and must step in and stop and monitor this new increased commercialization of the games.

In the end, our human love for skilled exertion, movement and bodily grace, our delight in stretching the human boundaries and in spontaneity, our intense interest in the drama of sports—these embodied, almost erotic qualities, lend to sport its capacity for excellence. When the cry rings out, 'Let the Olympic games begin', it is these qualities we will want to celebrate in Seoul.

Note that this Special Column, like others in this series, is written under the sole responsibility of the author.

DIAKONIA: CHURCH FOR OTHERS

Norbert Greinacher
Norbert Mette

'The Churches' Return to Diakonia': Legacy and Task

'THE FATE of the Churches in coming times will not depend on what their prelates and leading authorities summon up in the way of intelligence, cleverness, "political capabilities" etc. It will depend on the Churches' return to diakonia: to the service of mankind. In fact to a service determined by mankind's need, not by our taste or by the consuetudinarium (the habits) of an ecclesiastical community, however well tried and tested. 'The son of man came not to be served but to serve" (Mark 10:45). The various realities of ecclesiastical existence need only be summoned once under that law and measured against that statement, and one really knows enough. No man will believe in the message of salvation and of the Saviour, if we have not worked ourselves to the bone in the service of man, whether he be sick in mind or body, in his social, economic or moral life, or whatever ...

Return to diakonia was what I said. By that I mean associating with man in all his situations, with the intention of helping him to master them, without afterwards filling up anywhere a column or a section. By that I mean going after mankind, following him even to where he is at his most forlorn and extreme, in order to be with him exactly where and when he is surrounded by what is forlorn and extreme. "Go forth", the Master said, and not: "Sit down and wait for someone to come." By that I mean concern too for human space and a humane order.'[1]

On 2 February 1945 Alfred Delp was executed. Even when faced with death he was saddened by how much and how exclusively Christians and Churches were occupied with their internal problems, so that they had thereby lost sight of the problems and needs of their fellow men. The further fate of the Churches, according to Delp, depends on whether they learn to disregard their small problems and perceive instead the huge problems facing their contemporaries. If they were however still capable of such a radical return to the attitude and practice of diaconate, was for Delp doubtful: 'The Churches here seem to be getting in their own way because of the nature of their historically hallowed way of life. I believe that if we do not, wherever possible, willingly abandon that way of life, for the sake of life, the history of here and now will strike us as a lightning bolt of judgement and destruction.'[2]

At almost the same time, in his prison cell, Dietrich Bonhoeffer had carried out, in key-word fashion, a stock-taking of Protestant theology in opposition to German National Socialism: 'Church in self-defence. No risk-taking for others.'[3] Thinking back to the 'existence-for-others' of Jesus,[4] he drew the famous conclusion: 'The Church is only the Church when it is there for others.'[5] What that meant for him in concrete terms, he formulated in the sentences following that remark: 'For a start it must give all property to those in need. Pastors must live exclusively on the voluntary gifts of parishes, possibly follow a secular profession. It must share in the secular tasks of mankind's communal life, not by dominating, but by helping and serving.'[6]

Devoted to man in his need, helping and serving him—these are, according to both these witnesses, the attributes of Churches walking the path of diakonia which is assigned them, and thereby taking leave of their conventional, historically hallowed way of life. 'Diakonia' means therefore more than an area of tasks derived from one of the basic ecclesiastical functions. It describes not only more or less a sector of ecclesiastical action, like the giving of alms and help for the helpless. But on its unconditional 'existence-for-others' rests the decision, as Bonhoeffer relentlessly reminds us, whether the Church is really Church or not, whether it therefore stands in the succession of him who, for his part, became and was 'the man for others.'[7] Christ's example is moreover not only the model and lasting yardstick of diaconate; but it is he himself who meets the Church in suffering human beings, robbed of their dignity, in the poor and the weak.

That God is on their side, that he is biased in their favour as a matter of priority, occurs as a basic experience and confession in the whole biblical tradition. Time and again it can therefore become a 'good message' precisely for the poor, as C. H. Abesamis explains in his contribution. How for instance in the practice and reflections of the early Church they tried to take this seriously, is substantiated, according to N. Brox, in numerous ancient ecclesiastical sources. However even in early times tendencies can be identified, as E. Schüssler-Fiorenza critically reminds us, where diakonia is allocated a place in the order of values beneath preaching the Gospel and church service, and deeds accorded a place beneath words and rites—a process, by the way, which to a large extent ran parallel to the expulsion of women from the ecclesiastical 'hierarchy'.

That was the start of a momentous and calamitous development: although impressive examples of Christian charity can be quoted for the whole course of Church history.[8] Right up to the present day, the Churches' commitment in the field of diakonia, particularly in fact where women are involved, is considerable. To some extent it has, in the meantime, experienced a differentiated expansion of its organisation in order thus to make more allowance for the conditions of an increasingly complex society with its diverse manifestations of need. The reverse of this development however is that, as a result of this commitment by individuals, groups or associations, awareness of the responsibility for diakonia has increasingly declined in the remaining areas of ecclesiastical practice. The consequences of this can be traced not least as far as the organisation of ecclesiastical office, in which (at least up to the Second Vatican Council) diaconate counted only as a preliminary stage of the 'real' priesthood. Within theology, diakonia was discussed, if at all, as a special theme of practical theology.

Recent times have however seen the beginnings of a reflection ont he 'diakonia emergency' (O. Fuchs) and the non-delegable 'diaconate of all believers' (J. Moltmann) in the theory and practice of pastoral work. The basic impetus for this came from the change of position effected by Christians and Churches in the 'Third World': a renunciation of their traditional presence among the privileged in favour of a priority option for the poor. Diakonia then no longer means—as H. Steinkamp demonstrates in comparison with the 'Church of the rich'—being intent on alleviating the sufferings of the poor and weak by providing caring assistance, but means instead a giving of oneself into the 'social focal points' and sharing life there with those affected. In the course of this unconditional support for their human dignity and rights and of the struggle in solidarity to achieve these, the Church experiences its identity anew. The outline of the parable of the Good Samaritan is further extended: 'It is not just a question of binding up wounds. It is also basically a question of exposing robbery and bringing it to an end. Attention to people in need and structural measures belong together.'[9] That means that diakonia cannot be restricted to individual assistance, however essential that is. But, proceedings from need in its concrete manifestations, there must be an enquiry into its structural causes—going as far as how they are interwoven on a world-wide scale. The article by A. Adedeji provides an informative and startling example of this. Where there is talk and action of this kind, diakonia inevitably becomes political and prophetic. Its partiality causes offence; but only by doing so can it provide the impetus to change one's own ways (cf., the contributions by F. Betto and P. Kalilombe).

This conversion to a 'Church of diakonia' has not been without effect on the pastoral theory and practice in the 'First World'. Here too the concern of the population not sharing in increasing prosperity, is growing ever greater (cf., the contribution by G. Baum). The Churches too have been affected by the spread of a segregation minded society, trying to cut groups of people off because they are felt by the community to be strange.[10] Whether the Churches with their sometimes imposingly developed diakonia, function only to compensate the victims of the prosperous society, or whether they are capable of providing a creative opposition to pathogenic political and economic developments, and of allowing the power of belief to establish relations to be experienced beyond social barriers, that has become for them a decisive challenge (cf., the contributions by O. Fuchs and N. Mette).

All the same it cannot be a question of the Churches setting themselves up in abstract contrast to the rest of society or state, but of championing a 'politics of compassion' *in* society (cf., the contribution by J. Degen). Return to diakonia does not mean a retreat by the Church from society, it means rather a greater awareness of how it is intertwined with society and thus learns to understand and practise its task as 'cultural diaconate' (cf. the contribution by G. Fuchs).[11]

Theology too cannot remain unaffected by the call for a return to diakonia. Whoever pleads for a 'diakonia from below' cannot any more wish to pursue a 'theology from above'. Diakonia cannot simply be classed as a special theme of Practical Theology. It must rather make itself felt as a dimension of all theology. That however also requires of theology an about-face, a 'downwards career' (H. Schürmann): knowing God means hearing the cry of the poor and weak and becoming their neighbour. This edition of CONCILIUM is intended to contribute to that. We hope thereby also to make a contribution to the 'World assembly of Christians for peace, justice and the preservation of creation' which we fully support.

The Churches' return to diaconate! How lastingly topical this exhortation is, was shown by the deliberations of the world conference 'Diakonia 2000—becoming neighbours', organised by the Commission for Inter-Church Assistance, Refugees and World Service (CICARWS) of the World Council of Churches in Larnaca (Cyprus); the self-commitment expressed in the final declaration points the way for a Church of diakonia: 'On the threshold of the third millennium we solemnly commit ourselves from this day forth to work for justice and peace through our diakonia. We commit ourselves to the realisation of a vision which allows us to identify and show solidarity with those who are in the midst of the struggle for a peace based on justice. Our present and future diakonia must be founded on mutual trust and genuine sharing with one another. We know that people and Churches on every continent have needs and that with our diakonia we must reach all those who suffer. We know too that the powers standing in our way are many and that the way before us is long and difficult. And we know that we cannot do less than take up the Cross, and follow the suffering Christ, our Lord, who serves all mankind. His victory over death gives us life and hope.'[12]

Translated by Gordon Wood

Notes

1. Alfred Delp, Jesuit and member of the resistance against German National Socialism, wrote the essay 'Das Schicksal der Kirchen' in prison between September 1944 and February 1945 with his hands bound. In: A. Delp *Gesammelte Schriften* ed. by R. Bleistein, Vol. IV (Frankfurt 1984) 318–323, here 318–320.

2. Ibid. 321.

3. D. Bonhoeffer *Widerstand und Ergebung* (new edition), (Munich [3]1985) 414.

4. See ibid.

5. Ibid. 415.

6. Ibid.

7. Ibid. 414.

8. See the surveys in C. Boff/J. Pixley *Die Option for die Armen* (Düsseldorf, 1987) 174–200; P. Philippi 'Diakonie. I. Geschichte der Diakonie' in *TRE VII* (1981) 621–544. See also H. Steinkamp's contribution to this edition.

9. F. Kamphaus *Der Preis der Freiheit* (Mainz 1987) 166; see also W. Dirks *Die Samariter und der Mann aus Samaria. Vom Umgang mit der Barmherzigkeit* (Freiburg, 1985).

10. See J. Moltmann *Diakonie im Horizont des Reiches Gottes* (Neukirchen-Vluyn 1984) 18.

11. Unfortunately it was not possible to include in this edition a contribution on the Churches' diakonia in a socialist society. Readers are therefore referred to the case-study by R. Turre 'Chancen und Probleme diakonischer Arbeit in der sozialistischen Gesellschaft'. In: *EvTh 45* (1985) 401–415.

12. From the 'Declaration of Larnaca'. In: epd-Dokumentation 3/87, 54ff., here 56.

PART I

Distress that calls to Heaven: Focus of Human Need

Adebayo Adedeji

A Divided World, Can We Escape Mutual Injury and Self-Destruction?

IMMEDIATELY AFTER the second World War, many people agreed that they had to build a better world on these foundations: *justice*, beginning with a new socio-economic order; *freedom*, especially political liberty resulting from the end of imperialism and colonialism; tolerance, particularly racial tolerance as well as an end to racism and racial prejudice; and *humanity*, especially in the shape of a universal recognition of the unity of humankind and of the dignity of human beings.

But yesterday's hopes have become today's disillusionment. The revolution brought about by the burgeoning expectations of the 1950's and 60's has turned into rebellious frustration. In the two last decades—and really since the end of the second World War—our world has remained split and disunited. Opponents confront one another on all sides: we have the opposition of the great power, ideological confrontation, and the confrontation of the owners of this world—of the industrial nations of the north—and of the dispossessed—the Third World nations of Latin America, Asia and Africa. Instead of people being their brothers' and sisters' keepers, we have to deal increasingly with egocentrism, self-seeking and cynicism. Sad to say, we live in a time of egotistical show. Behind that show an ever greater number of people and of nations pursue an intense self-interest which, to an extent hitherto unknown, and especially on an international level, blinds them to what communal life and the social order really demand from each individual in every country.

1. A RETURN TO BLINKERED THOUGHT

It is undeniable tht the world today is more interdependent than ever before. The range and complexity of political, economic, cultural and social relations between the states and peoples of our earth have increased to an extraordinary degree in the last forty years. This is especially true of the first two and a half decades after the second World War, when all societies showed a firm tendency to internationalism. The western nations worked together in an exemplary manner to reconstruct the national economies of Europe which had been destroyed by war, and on an international scale unique progress was clearly made in the creation of riches and income.

This cooperation and internationalism lasted only a generation. Inasmuch as the difference between the rich north and poor south became a deep gulf, cooperation decreased and was finally replaced by confrontation. Successive economic crises with low or zero growth rates in the north and corresponding mass unemployment led to a blinkered self-centredness in the industrial nations. Under these conditions cooperation between north and south was drastically reduced. Economic nationalism is once again a distateful reality in a world whose economic interdependence is greater than before.

The dangers inherent in the present crisis of international relations and the world economy grow more acute day by day. In the long term the gulf between north and south is not in our interest. It is becoming clearer every day that local problems have international repercussions and therefore can be solved only on an international level. In other words: since the international system has become much more complicated and interdependent, apparently domestic political problems, such as the environment, energy, currency, trade, finance and employment, can be solved only by international cooperation. The economic situation of a country depends increasingly on the achievements and behaviour of other countries. The North-South Commission's report repeatedly states that 'the south cannot develop appropriately without the north and the north cannot flourish or improve its situation if there is no greater progress in the south'.[1] In his introduction to the report, Willy Brandt says very aptly: 'Whether it suits us or not, we are increasingly faced wth problems which affect mankind as a whole, so that consequently the solutions too have—increasingly to be internatinalised. The globalisation of dangers and demands—war, chaos, self-destruction—demands a kind of 'inner world politics which extends far beyond the horizon of self-interest but also of national frontiers. To date this has occurred only at a snail's pace. A defensive pragmatism prevails far and wide at a time when the true interests of mankind demand now perspectives and farsighted leadership'.[2]

2. THE GUILT PROBLEM AND ITS CONSEQUENCES

In view of the extent, and the present relevance, of the guilt problem, I should like to treat it in somewhat greater detail. Whatever the reasons why the developing nations have incurred such horrendous debts to the other countries, one of the most consequential effects is the return of capital from poor to rich nations. Since 1945 and with the start of Marshall Aid, development has meant alsmost exclusively the flow of means from the industrial nations to the Third World.

This was also the case in the nineteenth century, and in the first one and a half decades of this century. With the beginning of the debt crises in 1982, this capital flow changed direction. The International Currency Fund, for example, has calculated that in 1985 alone the seven most heavily indebted world debtor nations (Brazil, Mexico, South Korea, Argentina, Venezuela, Indonesia and the Philippines) paid a total of 32,000 million US dollars to their lenders: that is, almost 20% of their total export earnings. In 1985 the interest payments alone of the developing countries amount to some 54,000 million US dollars.

The foreign debts of the African nations are wholly quantitative, but amount to much less than those of the big seven. Nevertheless, they are a far greater burden on these national economies, since they are so underdeveloped that even servicing the interest is beyond them. In 1977, the interest payments of the African nations as a whole were some 12% of their export earnings. In 1985 they were already above 30%. Such average figures nevertheless say little about the situation of individual countries such as, for example, Sudan and Zaïre, whose interest payments are some 40–70% of their export earnings. Hence considerable sums flow back even from Africa, which is extremely poor, and it is forseeable that they will rise further in years to come.

This return of money—however unnatural and injurious to the world economy it may be—is often described by official circles in the industrial nations—which are not prepared to acknowledge their co-responsibility for the operation of the world economy—as a 'necessary adaptation'. We can only agree with Harold Lever and Christopher Huhne when they say that it is a matter of urgency to get to grips with the debt problem, both because it represents a danger—and because it is symptomatic of a profound inadequacy of the West. Over the last 20 years we have observed a continued crystallisation of the reluctance of the western democracies to adjust to the growing interdependence of the world economy. Those who control universal destinies—politicians, civil servants, currency experts, and so on—have shown that they are incapable of thinking strategically. Urgent deferred problems are tackled in an uncoordinated way without any sense of long-term planning. The method of treating each instance as it comes along (which is certainly justified on some occasions) is interpreted as an inclusive principle. In fact it is a sign of intellectual bankruptcy and is intended to hide the reality of attempting to escape responsibility for the results of ones own actions. The policy is one of asking others to trust them in regard to market mechanisms, as if the money market existed in a vacuum and was not controlled by the major financial organisation[3] to a very considerable extent.

In the foregoing I have concentrated on the debt crisis, but we should not forget that if it is certainly the biggest, it is by no means the sole economic problems which now confronts the international community. Here I shall restrict myself to a description of three other problems: international trade, currency policy, and balance of payment deficits.

3. FAMINE, INADEQUATE NUTRITION, POVERTY: THE SCANDAL OF SUFFERING

At the very start of her very readable, courageous and inspiring book on the fundamental causes of famine, Susan George compares the current political and economic world order with the social-class conditions of individual countries in nineteenth century Europe, and the present day Third World with the nineteenth century working class. She says that all the images of horror, which we now look back on with a mixture of revulsion and disbelief, have a mirror-image (and worse) in the countries of present-day Asia, Africa and Latin America. There are more than 500 million people live in conditions which the World Bank terms 'absolute impoverishment'. Just as the property-owning classes of earlier times opposed all reform, and foretold the imminent danger of an economic catastrophe if it was forbidden to employ eight-year-olds in factories, today the exploiters of poverty, who are responsible for hunger, try to maintain the *status quo* between the rich and poor worlds.[4]

Ten years after the publication of George's book, the members of the 'Project Hunger' group were strongly committed as individuals and together in the struggle to free our planet before the end of the century from hunger and an inadequate diet. They issued a seminal text.[5] It describes facts and contexts which are so appealing that they could not but arouse the conscience of the rich world, if it had not become so very hard and cynical. I shall cite only a few examples. Whereas the industrial nations complimented themselves on the fact the harvests race ahead of population growth, and for the first time in the world's history more food is being produced than the world needs',[6] every year 13–18 million people die of hunger. That is an average of 35,000 people a day and 24 people a minute—18 of them children. About 1,000 million people, a fifth of the human race, are chronically or acutely undernourished.

No other kind of catastrophe has so devasting effect as famine. In the last two years it has swallowed up as many sacrificial victims as both world wars combined. The 'famine belt' stretches from South East Asia over the Indian sub-continent, the Middle East and Africa, to the equatorial zone of Latin America. The North-South Commission was quite justified when it said: 'The idea of a United Nations is rather meaningless when famine ... is treated as a marginal problem which the human race can manage to live with'.[7] We must also remember that it is relatively easy to get rid of hunger, whereas it is much more difficult to remove the results of malnutrition and undernourishment.

4. ARMAMENT COSTS AND THEIR SOCIAL DUES

The burdens and waste bound up with the arms race, its harmful effects on the world economy and its social costs have by now reached astronomical sums—insofar as they are even calculable. According to a UNO report to 1985 the worldwide arms expenditure in 1983 reached some 750 milliard US dollars: that is, 150 US dollars for every man, woman, and child. That is more than the average per capital income in many developing countries.[8] Compared with the sums which we devote to armaments all over the world, development expenditure is negligible. State development aid amounts annually to 30 milliard US dollars, the real value of which drops, whereas arms expenditure is forty times higher and constantly rising. Humankind has not yet grasped the simple but very important fact that more weapons make the world poorer not safer.

As the North-South Commission noted correctly in their first report, there is a moral link between the immense expenditure on armaments and the ludicrously small expenditure on measures intended to stop hunger and sickness in the Third World. The World Health Organisation programme for malaria detection is short of cash. Estimates put its cost at 450 million dollars—which would be only a thousandth of the annual world expenditure for military purposes. The cost of a ten-year programme to cover the most important nutritional and health needs in the developing countries would cost less than a half of annual arms expenditure.[9]

Of course, by far the greatest part of arms expenditure is the responsibility of both superpowers and their associates. But many Third World arms expenditure rose twice as fast as that of the industrial nations. Therefore it is hardly surprising that since 1945 there have been in the Third World about 150 small and larger armed conflicts, which have killed at least 16 (but probably some 20) million people. Thus in a forty-year period between 33,000 and 41,000 people have been slaughtered each month[10]

The arms-exporting nations of the industrialised North give development aid reluctantly but are only too willing to provide the southern nations with weapons. Of course the developing nations want weapons to guarantee their security; yet—just as much as the super-powers and the other northern countries—eventually they will have to acknowledge that their nations are made not safer but poorer—very much poorer—by arms. Moreover those who sell arms to the developing nations bear moral and political responsibility for the growing impoverishment of the South.

5. INCREASING SPREAD OF RACISM RACIAL PREJUDICE AND DISCRIMINATION

'In Christ there is no east or west.
In him no south or north,
But one great fellowship of love,
Throughout the whole wide earth.'

This and similar hymns are gladly sung with—so it seems, anyway—conviction by Christians all over the world. They depend on a basic Christian teaching: that is, that before God there is neither Jew nor heathen, neither black nor white. Yet today's Christian world features racism and racial discrimination, and a host of racial prejudices and tensions. People do not reat one another as human beings, as equally entitled common members of the human community. They treat one another as Jews and Arabs, as blacks and whites, as Christians and Muslims. In the 2,000 years since the birth of our Lord, and especially in the last 300 years, racism has become a swollen tumour in the body of humankind. Countless crimes and acts of violence are committed in Christ's name. Even among Christians and in Christian countries, we have not yet achieved a north-south dialogue, but the north has refused to favour the south in Christ, and white Christians have not thought it necessary to treat their 'coloured' and 'black' fellow Christians with care, respect and brotherly love.

The worst instance of racism since the Nazi Holocaust is the apartheid system, which is directed against the black and coloured inhabitants of South Africa. In the first case millions of Jews were exterminated. In addition, vast numbers of people were persecuted, and tortured, deprived of their civic rights and exposed to all kinds of humiliating and brutal treatment, as they have been under apartheid. The extent and nature of both systems show how fundamentally wicked and evil human beings are. But it is yet more distressing that in both cases Christians have done nothing on seeing crimes committed in the name of racial superiority.[11]

The apartheid system is shameful, but we should not behave as if there were racism only in South Africa. It exists in some form almost everywhere. If we do not succeed in banishing apartheid and all forms of racial discrimination and racial prejudice, then the existence of our civilisation will be at stake.

6. THE TRAGEDY OF REFUGEES AND DISPLACED PERSONS

One of the results of growing racism and intolerance is the flood of refugees—people who have left their homelands voluntarily or by compulsion. We all agree that the behaviour of the individual partly depends on his or her potentialities for achieving life goals, expectations and hopes. If human living and working conditions promote human development and self-confidence, then people will usually consent to the social order in which they live. But if people live under conditions which are generally discouraging, then they will easily become prey to frustrations and problems, turn introverted and even become alienated. It may be impermissibly simplistic to say so, but our world seems to me to be split into two 'psychological' camps. On one side, there are the countries in which there is a genuine equality of opportunity in spite of all racial, religious or sex differences; and on the other hand there are those which in spite all rhetoric or political solutions do not recognise such equality of opportunity. In the first case the individual develops a positive attitude to his or her environment; in the second case he or she loses all interest, especially in public instances, and tries by every means, but with as little effort as possible, to achieve as must as possible. Corruption flourishes under such conditions. In those societies where the development and participation of the individual are not promoted, in which there is no freedom but rather repression—no equality of opportunity but rather repression; where human dignity and human rights are not respected, but fundamentally and brutally denied; where the development of the individual depends not on his or her abilities, but on colour of skin, people seek refuge elsewhere.

In terms of the total world community, the number of people who have left their homelands is alarming. There are ten million refugees, and according to conservative estimates some 19.57–21.7 million people live as foreign labourers in countries other than their homelands. All these people are faced with numerous problems. They meet increasingly with rejection and even enmity, above all in countries where a poor economic situation, unemployment, discrimination and racist attitudes lead to a reduced intake capacity. In Africa, population shifts in recent years have reach alarming dimensions. Fifty per cent of all refugees (some 5 million) now live in Africa, which has the superhuman task of supporting millions of people who have had to leave the drought regions (the number of those displaced persons in African countries who are at the limits of drought and famine is estimated at 10 million), and at the same time has to solve the complex problems of nomad labour (estimated at 2 million people). I believe that here, compared with all the other continents, we are exceptionally privileged, in the sense of our solidarity with displaced persons. We neither check nor restrict population shifts within and between countries. We accept the displaced and share with them. But what we share with them is above all poverty, for the little we have is perilously reduced. And yet—our attitude to the fate of our fellow humans in the present-day world in which there is so much indifference, self-seeking and egotism, has clearly become rather rare.

7. THE WORLD IN AD 2000

Today our world is at the crossroads. Since the end of the second world war, it has become more interdependent than ever before and yet it grows increasingly divided. Whereas today, thanks to scientific and technological progress, it has become physically much smaller than two decades ago or even one decade ago, the gulf between the industrial and the developing nations becomes wider every day. Nowadays we speak of one world, yet we are more divided than ever before—by ideological differences, by our differing ideas of the nature of our relations, and above all by our unequal opportunities of creating additional wealth, of controlling our natural resources and our environment, and of satisfying the needs—sometimes the most elementary needs—of the population of our particular country. Whereas our world as a whole is richer and better-off than ever before, and whereas the standard of living since 1945 has risen rapidly and the quality of life has improved, it is clear that this development affects only a small part of our planet—the industrialised nations of the OECD and COMECON. For two-thirds of humankind, who live in Asia, Latin America and Africa, and are known collectively as the Third World—life is still short and harsh. This applies especially to Africa, where millions of children die of malnutrition even as infants, where hundreds of thousands are inadequately clothed, miserably housed and scarcely supplied with the bare necessities of life.

Unfortunately there is no sign of any possible major change in this order of things between now and the year 2000. If there is any indication at all, it is of developments which would probably make the situation even more pressing. I shall spend a short time on three such developments.

First: the speedy population growth will continue at a dramatic rate far into the third millenium. The world population has risen dramatically in the twentieth century. In 1900 there were less than 2,000 million people. By the year 2000 there will be 5,000 million. The population growth will be most rapid in the Third World, most especially in Africa. It is thought that Africa, which in 1960 was estimated at a population of 257 million, will contain about 1,000 million people in the year 2000. Thus Africa's share of the world's population will rise from 8–10% in the 1960s to 20% in AD 2000.

The second factor, which will probably lead to a very much worse situation by the start of the next millenium, concerns the load on the ecological system, the injurious effects of which are becoming apparent all over the world. There is no doubt that 5,000 million people represent an immense burden on the world eco-system. The growing lack of agriculturally useful terrain, the pollution of the biosphere by heavy industry, and the continual harm to the environment, will probably be decisive problems in the next millenium. The fateful interaction between fast population growth and the danger of the co-system will probably be most unfortunate in Africa, where excessive agricultural exploitation of the earth, transfer, and deforestation will probably hasten the process of dessertification and lead more often to drought.

Third: the already fast growth of technological development in the last forty years before the next millenium will probably proceed at an even faster rate. This speedy advance of technology will probably be accompanied by a heavy concentration of advanced technology in the hands of the superpowers, so that the rest of the world to varying degrees will be practically forced to import their technology. I hardly need remark that the technological gap between North and South will have increased even more by then, and access to technology and technology transfer will be more difficult, if not quite impossible.

Even with space travel and exploitation of seabed resources, there are problems and potential dangers. We can hardly overemphasise the technological implications of these two areas and the exploitation of such enterprises is scarcely to be underestimated. Can they really be justly distributed? Will it be possible in this regard to avoid domination, exclusive rights and overrule? Space research should not be equated with control of space, and the treasures of the seabed, which belong to the human heritage, should not be reserved for those with the means to explore and exploit them. The planet and its space are there for all humankind: for the rich and the poor, the powerful and powerless, the developed and the developing. Finally, the threatened danger of a worldwide holocaust will further menace the human race, but it will, one hopes, remain only a threat, and humankind wll be spared destruction. That can happen if the present hatred and distrust of the two superpowers and the apparent antithesis of their political and economic goals is replaced with understanding, tolerance and cooperation.

8. THE RESPONSES AND RESPONSIBILITY OF CHRISTIANS

What answer are we as Christians to give to those—major and very disquieting—demands which face us as the second millenium approaches its end and the third lies before us?

Historically, the Church has concerned itself more with the formulation of creeds and liturgies which proclaim personal salvation, than with Jesus's social commandments, which have to do with our duty of love of our neighbours. As long as we as Christians do not stoutly and without reservation accept that we are our brothers' and sisters' keepers, as long as we do not acknowledge our common being as human, and do not put into action our belief that all people, whatever their race, are created equal and with the same right to life, freedom and striving for happiness, our faith will remain a flight from the demands that Jesus Christ himself expressed two thousand years ago.

Of course the Church must keep to its commission to save souls. But it should also recognise as no less important a task the duty of being in the very vanguard of the struggle against the brutal oppression and exploitation of people by other people, and of one race and one nation by other nations. Since in Christ there are neither slaves nor free, and therefore no reasons for the domination of part of humankind by another, the Church will have to play a more positive and bolder prophetic role, when it is a matter of persuading the governments and people of all countries, especially Christian countries, to move closer to Christ and to allow him to guide their public discourse and action. The ecumenical movement has to inspire people all over the world to realise the ineluctable necessity of practising neighbourly love on a worldwide scale, and of making and improving social political and economic ties which will express that love, and produce mutual understanding, among various religious sects and ideologies, so that cooperation rules instead of contention, understanding instead of distrust, and love instead of hatred.

As Christians, we have to be in the vanguard of the practice of neighbourly love. As the Church of Christ, we have to show that we are not only fighting for the redemption of souls, but that we are also struggling with all our might for a better quality of human life here on earth. With some honourable exceptions, the churches have been lacking when it was a question taking up a position in regard to the major problems of our time. The Church should play a more prophetic role and accuse prophetically.

Fundamentally, I should like to state tht the Church ought to play a new role as the advocate and protector of democracy; justice—especially economic and social justice: tolerance—especially racial tolerance and the destruction of racism and racial prejudice; humanity—especially the humanity of a universal support of the ideal of humanity; and peace, that is, true peace and not a mere balance of terror.

Then, perhaps, the new heaven and new earth promised in the Bible will not remain mere wishful thinking and Utopia.

Translated by J. C. Cumming

Notes

* This article is a version by the editorial committee responsible for this issue of Concilium of the keynote paper which Dr Adebayo Adedeji gave at the world conference 'Diakonia 2000' (held by the Commision for Interchurch Aid, Refugee and World Service of the WCC) on 19 November 1986 at Larnaca (Cyprus). The full text appears under the title 'On the Threshhold of the 3rd Millenium and the 21st Century—Can our world escape Mutual Hurt and Self-destruction?' in *epd-Documentation* No. 3/87, pp. 1–24.

1. *Dass Überleben sichern. Gemeinsame Interessen der Industrie und Entwicklungsänder* (report of North-South Commission with Willy Brandt as Chairman; Cologne 1980), 45.

2. Ibid. 27.

3. H. Lever & C. Huhne *Debt and Danger* (Boston & New York 1985) ix, 141.

4. S. George *Wie die anderen sterben* (Berlin 1980).

5. Cf *Ending Hunger: an idea whose time has come* (New York 1985).

6. K. Schneider 'Scientific Advances Lead to Era of Food Surplus around the world' in *The New York Times* (9.9.1986).

7. *Das Uberleben sichern, op. cit.*, 116.

8. *1985: On the World Social Situation* UN Sales Publications No. E 85, IV.2, 16.

9. *Das Überleben sichern op. cit.*, 149ff.

10. *1985 Report on the World Social Situation, op. cit.*, 14.

11. In no way do I wish to undervalue the untiring and sometimes sacrificial attempts of individual Christians in Western Europe and North America to support those who are affected by this pointless and brutal persecution and who are deprived of their human dignity. I am much more distressed by the attitude of the populations and governments of these countries.

Gregory Baum

Victims in the Affluent Society

1. VICTIMS IN NORTH AMERICAN SOCIETY

PEOPLE in the USA and Canada readily recognise conditions of oppression in Third World countries and hence have great sympathy for the theology of liberation. Yet many of these think that North American society offers equality of opportunity and hence allows those who work hard to improve their economic condition. While there are signs of injustice here and there, these people believe that it would be overly dramatic and hence slightly exaggerated to speak of 'victims' in this society. There is no place, according to them, for a liberation theology in the developed countries.

Are these North Americans right? Is their perception of their own society valid? The same question arises in the European welfare capitalist countries. Can one speak of 'the victims' of these societies? To find an answer to this question we must engage in dialogue with social scientists. It is their task to analyse the structure of society and estimate its impact on the population at all levels.

Yet social scientists are not in agreement on this issue. Their answer depends in large measure on the methodology they employ in their investigation. Some study society as a functioning organism in equilibrium and hence regard patterns of exclusion and discrimination as temporary phenomena about to be corrected by reforms summoned forth by these oppressive conditions. Other social scientists begin their study of society by focusing on the people at the bottom and in the margin, and then turn to an analyses of the conditions in that society that have caused the exclusion of these people from participation. The choice of method in social science is not free of value-implications.

The Church is deeply concerned about the social evil in the region to which it belongs. Pope Paul VI asked that 'Christian communities analyse with objectivity the situation proper to their country'.[1] Dialogue with social science is here inevitable. A wide network of Christians in North America have engaged in such dialogue. They have come to an understanding of their society by listening first of all to the people at the bottom and in the margin. Eventually the Catholic bishops of the USA and Canada have offered their own critical social analysis.

In this article, I wish to present the Catholic bishops' understanding of oppression and marginalisation in North America. I could have gone directly to the social science literature. Yet I regard it as highly significant that the Catholic bishops, following a minority movement in their churches, have committed themselves to a radical social analysis of their societies. In a recent document, the Canadian bishops render a systematic account of their pastoral methodology, the first steps of which deal with the analysis of social evil. Here is the text.

'This pastoral methodology involves a number of steps:

(i) being present with and listening to the experiences of the poor, the marginalised, the oppressed in our society (e.g., the unemployed, the working poor, the welfare poor, Native peoples, the elderly, the handicapped, small producers, racial and cultural minorities, etc.); (ii) developing a critical analysis of the economic, political, and social structures that cause human suffering; (iii) making judgements in the light of Gospel principles and the social teaching of the Church concerning social values and priorities.'[2]

Since the next two steps deal with the Church's positive response to the conditions of oppression, they are not relevant to this article which deals exclusively with the definition of society's victims. When the Canadian bishops speak of Gospel principles and the Church's social teaching in this context, they refer above all to two principles, 'the option for the poor' and 'the priority of labour over capital.'[3] In other words, they evaluate society in general in terms of its effect on the poor and powerless, and they evaluate the economic system in particular in terms of the service it renders to the workers, to the great majority, to the people.

While the Canadian bishops, in dialogue with the other Canadian Churches, have developed their radical social analysis over a period of more than a decade and expressed it in a many succinct pastoral messages, the American bishops adopted the option for the poor as their entry into social analysis for the first time in their extensive pastoral letter on the US economy in 1986. In the following pages I shall first present elements of analysis offered by the American bishops and then move very briefly to the social analysis of the Canadian bishops which ends up in an ethical critique of the capitalist economy.

2. THE AMERICAN PASTORAL

The American bishops explicate the biblical and theological foundation of their approach which they also sum up in the expression, 'the option for the poor.'[4] Like the Canadian bishops they analyse the social condition of their society by focusing on the victims. In capitalist countries such an analysis begins with a study of the materially deprived, i.e., with the economically disadvantaged, and from there moves to an examination of the cultural and spiritual consequences of economic oppression. The American bishops chose to limit themselves to a few topics, the unemployed, the poor, agricultural workers, and dependent Third World peoples.

The bishops lament the increasing rate of unemployment. This development is accompanied, they say, by a new social theory that regards high unemployment as normal and natural, as something to which society will have to get accustomed. Since following Catholic social teaching, the bishops understand work as a human right, they regard high unemployment as a social evil and the unemployed as the victims of society. The Pastoral analyses the impact of joblessness on human lives and human dignity. It reviews the self-doubt and despair produced by unemployment, the devastating impact on family life, and the cultural changes in society as a whole. The scarcity of jobs heightens the spirit of competition. Working people become rivals rather than allies. High unemployment, moreover, allows management to increase the demands made on workers and create conditions that make work more burdensome and more alienating. This has a dehumanising effect on a large sector of society. And since the society wants to keep a good conscience, we witness the emergence of cultural trends that persuade people to blame the victims for being unemployed. Those without jobs are supposedly unreliable, maladjusted, lazy or cantankerous. The American bishops make the point, also emphasised by the Canadian bishops, that high unemployment not only damages the unemployed; it damages society as a whole. Society becomes harsher, more competitive, more frightened, more divided, more unwilling to look at itself realistically and hence more vulnerable to ideologies that disguise the true situation.

The American bishops go so far as to say that the manner in which a society organises its economy affects what people hope for themselves and their loved ones, what they envisage for their neighbours, and how they act together in society: 'it influences their very faith in God'.[5]

The American Pastoral then turns to an analysis of poverty in the United States. They recognise that poverty can be defined in different ways. If one makes the extreme deprivation experienced in certain developing nations the norm, then poverty is largely absent in the developed nations. If one defines poverty primarily in spiritual terms, as this is done by reactionary Catholic groups in the United States, then it refers to those who are estranged from God whether they be materially poor or rich. The American Pastoral defines poverty as the lack of material resources required for a decent life.[6] Material injustice creates spiritual poverty in the whole of society.

Poverty exists among the employed and the unemployed. Poverty is not an isolated problem affecting a few people in the large cities; it is a massive phenomenon present in all parts of the country and affecting people in different walks of life. Yet poverty strikes some groups more than others. Most distressing is the growing number of children who are poor. The number of children who are poor in the USA rose by four million between 1973 and 1983. 'Today one in every four American children under the age of 6 and one in every two black children under 6 are poor.'[7] A wealthy, developed society that allows such conditions to exist is spiritually deprived and in need of conversion.

An analysis of poverty in society refutes the popular myth of equal opportunity. The Pastoral focuses in particular on poverty among women and among the so-called racial minorities. In an earlier draft, the bishops used the provocative expression, 'the feminisation of poverty',[8] to designate the changes in the structure of poverty and the economic impact of anti-feminist discrimination. For instance, among the ever increasing number of households headed by women, i.e., families supported by the mother's income, the poverty rate is 33 per cent. Among minority families headed by women the poverty rate is over 50 per cent. A major factor behind this development is the wage discrimination against women. 'Women who work outside their homes full time and year round earn only 61 per cent of what men earn.'[9] Having a full time job is for women not a remedy for poverty. The pastoral shows that economic oppression of women affects anti-feminist discrimination in other areas and that women are indeed victims in modern society.

It is worth mentioning that several American and Canadian bishops have written pastoral statements which recognise the women's movement as a justice cause—something the Roman magisterium has not yet done—and reveal the impact of feminist theology on the North American hierarchy. Allow me to quote from the recommendation offered to the 1983 World

Synod of Bishops by Archbishop Vachon in the name of the Canadian bishops.

> 'In Canada an increasing number of women are speaking out and revealing their thoughts and feelings. The dualist vision of flesh and spirit and the sexist prejudices resulting from it have strongly marked their past and continue to mark their present, identifying them with "the occasion of sin". They have experienced and continue to experience alienation, marginalisation and exclusion in many forms. As for us, let us recognise the ravages of sexism and our own male appropriation of Church institutions and numerous aspects of the Christian life ... In our society and in our Church man has come to think of himself as the sole possessor of rationality, authority and active initiative, relegating women to the private sector and dependent tasks. Our recognition, as Church, of our own cultural deformation will allow us to overcome the archaic concepts of womenhood which have been inculcated in us for centuries.'[10]

An analysis of society's victims must include women. In every oppressed group or class, in the developed and the developing societies, the heavier burdens are always placed on women. While certain women's organisations in modern society concentrate mainly on the discrimination experienced by middle class women, the feminist movement as such, identifying with women everywhere and in all societies, creates solidarity with the poor and oppressed: for this, alas, is where the majority of women are located.

Let us return to the American Pastoral. Still in the chapter on poverty it offers an analysis of the economic situation of blacks and other visible minorities in the United States. 'While one out of every nine white Americans is poor, one of every three blacks and native Americans and more than one of every four Hispanics are poor.'[11] These figures record the economic impact of racism. And racism, according to the US bishops, is a sin, 'a sin that divides the human family, blots out the image of God among specific members of that family and violates the fundamental human dignity of those called to be children of the same Father'.[12]

The American Pastoral also examines the lot of farmers and farm workers in America. Recent developments have created a crisis situation in agriculture. The United States entered the 20th century with the ownership of productive land widely distributed. What has happened over the last decades is the ever increasing concentration of land ownership and consequently the loss of farms and the exodus of farmers from the land, the decline of rural communities, and the growing difficulties of the remaining family farms to survive. America is faced with the possible loss of an entire way of life. These changes are accompanied in some regions by massive rural unemployment and in others by exploitative working conditions on the large farming enterprises inflicted on labourers belonging largely to visible minorities. The Pastoral also examines government policy regarding food prices and farm subsidies to gain a better understanding of the plight of farm people today.

Finally the American Pastoral turns to the impact of the US economy on the peoples of the developing countries. In the past people thought they could come to an understanding of their society by studying what happened within its borders. This is still a presupposition entertained by many sociologists. The American bishops try to correct this. Because developed societies, and more especially super-powers, have an economic and political influence in many parts of the world, social observers cannot arrive at an understanding of these societies unless they look beyond the national boundaries and study the impact and possibly the domination exercised by these societies in other parts. To define who are the victims of American society, the Pastoral examines the role of the US in the global economy, in particular its influence through development assistance, trade, foreign private investment, the control of finance, food and price policies, and government foreign policy. The bishops conclude that 'the international economic order, like many aspects of our own economy, is in crisis: the gap between rich and poor countries and between rich and poor people within countries is widening. The United States represent the most powerful single factor in the international economic equation'.[13] In this context, an earlier draft of the Pastoral quoted a sentence uttered by Pope John Paul II on his 1984 visit to Canada: 'The poor people and poor nations of the South—poor in different ways, not only lacking food, but also deprived of freedom and other rights—will sit in judgment on the people of the rich North who take these goods away from them, amassing for themselves the imperialistic monopoly of economic and political supremacy at the expense of others'.[14]

In their Pastoral the American bishops are also mindful of other victims of American society. They briefly refer to youth left without guidance, the neglected elderly, the retarded and the handicapped. The same church document also offers daring proposals to overcome some of these injustices. It provides a new imagination for thinking about economic issues. Yet in this article we simply focus on the definition of society's victims.

3. THE CANADIAN BISHOPS

While the American bishops produced a book-length pastoral on the economy, the final version of which appeared in 1986, the Canadian bishops published a series of short pastoral messages, beginning over ten years ago, in which they applied their critical methodology. They arrived at essentially the same analysis of society's victims as did the American bishops. They began their analysis by examining economic deprivation and exploitation in Canada, then they turned to racist and sexist discrimination and examined their economic consequences. They analysed the structures of material injustices in society and then revealed the cultural and spiritual effects of these structures. With the American bishops they argued that social evil or social sin not only damaged the victims, the marginalised, the poor, it also damaged the more fortunate sector of society. A society that allows its institutions to produce such a gravely unjust distribution of wealth and power will generate a humanly restrictive culture, a culture that makes the victims invisible, that makes preoccupation with one's own success morally respectable, that reconciles people with social inequality, that persuades people that there is no humane alternative to capitalism, and that blesses the increasingly coercive measures necessary to preserve the social peace.

What is new and bold in the Canadian church documents is that they try to analyse the causes of these recent developments, in particular the change in the structure of capital.[15] The bishops argue that the relatively benign phase of welfare capitalism, that began in Canada after World War II, has come to an end. During this phase, the capitalists honoured an unwritten contract with society, assuring full employment, welfare legislation, and respect for labour organisations.

Since the Seventies, the bishops argue, capital has increasingly emancipated itself from society. To maximise profit and power, capital has undergone important changes. (*i*) *Capital is becoming international.* It shifts its industries to parts of the world where labour is cheap and where governments prohibit labour from organising. (*ii*) *Capital is becoming more concentrated.* Buying out the smaller and medium-sized enterprises, the larger corporations assume giant size. Their control of the economy is so powerful that government must serve their interest. (*iii*) *Capital is becoming more centralised.* To increase profitability industrial, commercial and financial institutions move closer together in certain metropolitan areas, which leads to economic decline and human suffering in the hinterland regions. (*vi*) *Capital is increasingly foreign owned.* In the Canadian context, the extraordinarily high degree of US ownership of the industries creates excessive dependency and economic vulnerability. Decisions regarding the future of Canadian workers are made by boards of directors in a foreign country that have no reason for solidarity with Canadian society. And (*v*) *the industries are becoming increasingly capital-intensive.* The new technology leads to massive cuts in employment.

What is taking place in Canada and in many parts of the developed world, the Canadian bishops say, is the beginning of a more cruel phase of capitalism. The policy of full employment has been abandoned, welfare legislation is increasingly reduced, and concerted efforts are made to harrass and humiliate labour organisations. Society is becoming more harsh. And this change in the structure of capital is accompanied by a new culture of selfishness, mentioned also by the American bishops, which reconciles the more fortunate with social inequality and suggests to the less fortunate that their lack of success is really their own fault.

What the Canadian bishops propose as remedy goes beyond the concern of this article. Briefly what they advocate is a politics of solidarity. They specify under the conditions of Canadian society the meaning of Pope John Paul's famous call for 'new movements of solidarity of the workers and with the workers'.[16]

Notes

1. *Octogesima adveniens* (1971) n. 4.
2. 'Ethical Reflections on Canda's Socio-Economic Order' n. 4. See E. F. Sheridan ed. *Do Justice!* (Toronto 1987) p. 412.
3. See G. Baum, D. Cameron *Ethics and Economics: Canada's Catholic Bishops on the Economic Crisis* (Toronto 1984) p. 44–51.
4. 'Economic Justice for All: Catholic Social Teaching and the US Economy' n. 52, *Origins: NC Documentary Service* 16 (27 November 1986) p. 418.
5. Ibid. n. 1, *Origins* p. 413.
6. Ibid. n. 173, *Origins* p. 429.
7. Ibid. n. 176, *Origins* p. 429.
8. First draft, *Origins* 15 (15 November 1984) p. 363.
9. American Pastoral, Final version n. 179, *Origins* 26 November 1986 p. 429.
10. See *The Ecumenist* 22 (January–February 1984) p. 31.
11. American Pastoral, Final version n. 181, *Origins* p. 430.
12. Ibid. n. 182, *Origins* p. 430.
13. Ibid. n. 90, *Origins* p. 440.
14. First draft, n. 318, *Origins* 14 (15 November 1984) p. 375.
15. See G. Baum, D. Cameron *Ethics and Economics* pp. 51–57.
16. *Laborem exercens* (1981) n. 8.

PART II

'I see the Distress of my People': Divine Compassion as a Christian Commission

Carlos Abesamis

Good News to the Poor

THERE IS one innocent little phrase which has not received its due attention in the two thousand years of Christian tradition but which is supremely important for us in the Third World today. I am referring to the phrase 'good news to the poor'. Let us examine various dimensions of this phrase.

1. ITS VARIOUS OCCURENCES

The following are its principal occurences:
' "Go and tell John what you hear and see: the blind receive their sight ... and *the poor have the good news proclaimed to them*".' (Matt. 11:4–5 and Luke 7:22–23)
' "The Spirit of the Lord is upon me, because he has anointed me *to preach (announce) good news to the poor*".'
' "Blessed are you *poor*, for yours is the *kingdom of God*".' (Luke 6:20).

2. MEANING OF 'GOOD NEWS TO THE POOR'

When Jesus said he was 'proclaiming good news to the *poor*', what poor was he referring to? The spiritually poor? Or the really, materially poor, that is, the 'poor, deprived and oppressed'? The latter would be people such as the beggars (Mark 10:46), casual workers (Matt. 20:1–9), tenants (cf., Matt. 21:33) and slaves (Matt. 8:6) that we meet in the gospel pages.

(a) Meaning of 'poor'

This is not the place to go into a lengthy exegetical argument. Rather I will draw attention to the use of the word 'poor' in Isaiah and in the gospels, and then come to a modest conclusion.

The *'anawim* or *'aniyim* of Isaiah is the background and inspiration for the 'poor' on Jesus' lips. The following are all the texts in Isaiah's writings in which he mentions the *'anawim* or *'aniyim*. These texts have to be read carefully to determine whether 'poor' (*'anawim* or *'aniyim*) refers to the spiritually poor or to the really poor, deprived and oppressed. Isa. 3:14; Isa. 10:1–2; Isa. 11:4; Isa. 14:32; Isa. 26:5–6; Isa. 29:19; Isa. 32:7; Isa. 41:17; Isa. 51:21–22; Isa. 54:11; Isa. 58:7; Isa. 61:1; Isa. 66:1–2.

We conclude in Isaiah, especially when he speaks of justice, liberation and joy, poor means, with one possible exception, the really poor rather than the 'spiritually poor'. More accurately, the Hebrew normally means 'oppressed'. Very frequently this oppression is due, as in the above contexts, to economic poverty. Thus the best translation for *'anawim* or *'aniyim*—at least in Isaiah— is 'poor, deprived and oppressed'. And this is the meaning that would jump out of the page as Jesus took up and read Isaiah.

The following are all the texts in the gospels in which 'poor' is mentioned. Mark 14:5–7 = Matt. 26:9–11; Mark 10:21 = Matt. 19:21 = Luke 18:22; Luke 14:13; Luke 14:21; Luke 16:19–22; Luke 19:8; Luke 21:1–4 = Mark 12:42; John 12:5–8; John 13:29; (Matt. 5:3). Plus the texts we are presently concerned with: Matt. 11:5 = Luke 7:22; Luke 4:18; Luke 6:20.

It is instructive that 'poor' in the gospels always means the really poor, except in one case when Matthew (Matt. 5:3) introduces the words 'in spirit' as an editorial modification. In other words, 'poor' in the gospels always refers to the really poor, unless it is qualified; and it is qualified only once, and not by Jesus but by Matthew!

We cannot, therefore, blithely say that when Jesus proclaimed good news to the *poor*, he was referring to the 'spiritually poor' or the 'poor in spirit'. We cannot narrowly limit—as we have often done in the Church—the poverty here to the 'poverty in spirit'. At the very least, Jesus must have referred (also) to the really, materially poor.

(b) Meaning of 'Good News'

In the phrase, 'good news to the poor', what does the 'good news' or Gospel consist in? Is it the good news about Jesus' sacrificial death for sin of which the poor will be the favoured beneficiaries? Not quite. Rather, the good news is the good news to the poor of any era: the Gospel of *justice* and their *liberation* from poverty and oppression! Proclaiming the Gospel to the poor is proclaiming liberation and justice.

3. JESUS' MISSION STATEMENTS

In theology and catechism, is 'proclaiming good news to the poor' considered part of Jesus' mission? Not much, it would seem. And so, it is worth meditating on the following key gospel texts.

'Now when John heard in prison abut the deeds of Christ, he sent word by his disciples and said to him, "Are you he who is to come, or shall we look for another?" And Jesus answered them, "Go and tell John what you hear and see: the blind receive their sight and the lame walk,lepers are cleansed and the deaf hear, and the dead are raised up, and *the poor have the good news proclaimed to them.*" ' (Matt. 11:2–5 = Luke 7:18–23).

'And he came to Nazareth ... he went to the synagogue ... the book of the prophet Isaiah ... where it was written, "The Spirit of the Lord is upon me, because he has anointed me *to preach good news to the poor*. He has sent me to proclaim release to the captives and recovering of sight to the blind, to set at liberty those who are oppressed, to proclaim the acceptable year of the Lord." And he closed the book ... And he began to say to them, "Today this scripture has been fulfilled in your hearing." ' (Luke 4:16–21).

We must recognise these texts for what they are. They are some of the principal 'mission-texts' in the gospels, i.e., texts which, by their context and tone,intend to tell the reader what Jesus' mission was. They are therefore very key texts in the gospels. Similarly, consider ' "Blessed are you poor, for yours is the kingdom of God." ' (Luke 6:20 = Matt. 5:3). In this statement there is an implied declaration of mission, i.e., the mission to proclaim the good news of the kingdom of God to the poor. Clearly this declaration comes from a person who was conscious of a certain mission. We can rightly call Luke 6:20 an indirect mission statement. And the sense and thrust of the statement is: 'I proclaim to the poor, deprived and oppressed the kingdom of God, which is the opposite of their poverty and oppression. Therefore, blessed are they.'

In conclusion, because 'Good news of justice and liberation for the poor' comes from very ancient tradition, most likely from Jsus himself, inspired by Isaiah's vision of future salvation,[1] is found in key mission-statements and is practically the one constant element mentioned in these key mission-statements. It certainly is quite central in Jesus' consciousness.

4. JESUS' ACTIONS

Mission-statements are merely statements. What about Jesus' *actions*? Were Jesus' actions good news to the poor, deprived and oppressed? In poverty-stricken Galilee, the multitudes (mostly the poor of the land attracted by a popular preacher and wonderworker) would have included the sick (malnourished and vulnerable to diseases), the possessed (many of whom were the mentally ill, victims of malnutrition and poverty) and many of the so-called 'sinners'. Besides the real sinners,[2] these so-called 'sinners' were people forced into sinful professions because of poverty (e.g., prostitutes and thieves) and the ignorant poor who did not know the Torah and were considered 'sinners' by the religious establishment.

Since the gospel pages portray Jesus as reaching out to the sick, the possessed, the crowds, the sinners, we can say that Jesus' actions and ministry were good news to the poor of his time.

Did Jesus' concern and care also go out to *non*-poor *outcasts*? Yes, of course, e.g., tax-collectors, lepers, children, women, possessed, sinners, the sick. These suffered from various forms of marginalisation: cultural, psychological, religious. Jesus cared for anyone who was suffering, oppressed or outcast. However, it does not seem wise to apply the word 'poor' to these outcasts, because biblical terminology reserves 'poor' (*'anawim*; *ptochoi*) to the really poor and oppressed. It is also the beginning of much confusion and rationalisation. It is therefore preferable to reserve 'poor' for the really poor and oppressed.

And what would Jesus' attitude be towards a rich outcast, e.g., a tax-collector? Jesus would care for him in so far as he is an ostracized tax-collector. But he would challenge him, in so far as he is rich, to sell what he has and give to the poor. (Cf. Mark 2:14; Mark 10:17–21; Luke 19:1–10.)

But did Jesus' actions effect substantial/structural liberation from poverty for the poor, deprived and oppressed? Jesus cared for the victims of oppression, but his actions as such, e.g. healings, cannot be said to bring them structural liberation. We should therefore look to other facets of his ministry, i.e., his teachings and action-teaching, for after all, one of Jesus' main roles was that of prophet-teacher.

5. JESUS' TEACHING

(a) Sayings of Jesus

Was Jesus' teaching something that would make the poor happy? Let us read carefully the following texts and see whether these prophetic utterances of Jesus would be a happy message to the poor. Mark 10:21; Luke 12:33–34; Luke 16:19–23; Matt. 6:24; Luke 6:21 and 24; Luke 12:15; Luke 12:16–21; Mark 10:23–25. These utterances of Jesus would certainly be pro-poor, critical of wealth and the wealthy and a happy message to the poor, deprived and oppressed.

(b) Jesus' teaching: substantial or structural liberation?

Can one say that Jesus' teaching offered (good news of) substantial and structural liberation and justice to the poor, deprived and oppressed? The following constitute Jesus' 'stand', 'platform' or 'philosophy' on such questions as 'possessions and poverty', 'social justice'. Mark 10:21; Luke 12:33–34.

And this is how the first Jesus-followers lived his teaching: Acts 2:42–47; Acts 4:32–35; Acts 4:36–37; (Acts 5:1–10 may also be read profitably) Matt. 23:23; Matt. 9:13; 12:7.

Let us first single out the words which have to do with 'possessions and poverty', 'social justice'

> Go, sell what you have, and give to the poor. (Mark 10:30)
> Sell your possessions, and give alms. (Luke 12:33–34)
> And all who believed were together and had all things in common; and they sold their possessions and goods and distributed them to all, as any had need. (Acts 2:42–47)
> No one said that any of the things which he possessed was his own, but they had everything in common.
> There was not a needy person among them, for as many as were possessors of lands or houses sold them, and brought the proceeds of what was sold and laid it at the apostles' feet; and distribution was made to each as any had need. (Acts 4:32–35)
> … sold a field which belonged to him, and brought the money and laid it at the apostles' feet. (Acts 4:36–37)
> … the weightier matters of the Law, justice and mercy and faith; these you ought to have done, without neglecting the others. (Matt. 23:23)
> 'I desire compassion, and not sacrifice.' (Matt. 9:13; 12:7)

(c) Jesus' stand on possessions and wealth

Jesus' stand on possessions and wealth was quite forthright and clear: 'give', 'distribute', i.e., *share*.

Go, sell what you have, and give to the poor (Mark 10:21) and *Sell your possessions, and give to the poor* (Luke 12:33) constitute Jesus' prophetic view of things. When this prophetic vision was translated into actual life, the kind of community that emerged in the Acts of the Apostles (Acts 2:42–47; 4:32–35) was one in which everyone had all things in common. Everyone sold their possessions and goods, like land and houses (from each according to his capacity) and distributed them to all, as any had need (to each according to his need). No one said that any of the things which he possessed was his own, and there was not a needy person among them.

Go, sell what you have, and give to the poor (Mark 10:21) and *Sell your possessions, and give to the poor* (Luke 12:33) constitute a prophetic view of things and not an economic programme, for Jesus was a prophetic figure rather than an economist. But if the spirit of this prophetic vision of Jesus were to provide the inspiration for an economic programme for contemporary society, what kind of human community would we have? What kind of social system would emerge? This is left to the readers to mull over and discuss.

Can we then say that Jesus' teaching on 'possessions and poverty' offer (good news of) substantial and structural liberation and justice to the poor, deprived and oppressed. It would seem so.

(*d*) Social justice?

Did Jesus teach anything which would amount to a demand for what we could call today 'social justice'? To understand Jesus, we must familiarise ourselves with a set of vocabulary at the heart of the teaching of the Israelite prophets. An Israel where there was social injustice—shedding of innocent blood, unjust laws and venal courts, oppression of the poor, widows, the fatherless—is an Israel where there was no *sedakah* (justice or righteousness), *mishpat* (justice or right), *hesed* (compassion, mercy or steadfast love) or *'emet* (truth, faithfulness). (See: Isa. 59:3–15; Isa. 1:21–23; Isa. 5:7.)

Salvation in the future means the presence of *sedakah, mishpat, hesed and 'emet*: Isa. 1:26–27; Isa. 9:6–7; Isa. 32:15–16; Isa. 33:5; Hos. 2:19–20.

From these texts, it is clear that *sedakah, mishpat, hesed and 'emet* mean social justice and are central to the message of the prophets.

What about Jesus? (Before answering this question, one would do well to make a mental list of things which would constitute 'the most important or weightier matters' in the Christian religion. Compare this with Jesus' list.) This is what *Jesus* had to say:

> Woe to you, scribes and Pharisees, hypocrites! for you tithe mint and dill and cummin, and have neglected the weightier matters of the Law, justice (*mishpat*) and (*hesed*) and faith (*'emet*); these you ought to have done, without neglecting the others. (Matt. 23:23)

Go and learn what this means, 'I desire compassion (*hesed*), and not sacrifice.' (Matt. 9:13; 12:7)

For Jesus, the more important things in religion are *sedakah, mishpat, hesed, 'emet*. Jesus then quite clearly taught something which would amount to a demand for 'social justice', as we would call it today. In fact, Jesus places *sedakah, mishpat, hesed, 'emet* at the heart of true religion (Matt. 23:23 and see Matt. 25:31–46). And, Jesus, like Yahweh, would rather have human justice than worship! (Matt. 9:13; Hos. 6:6)

Knowing Jesus' 'stand' or 'philosophy' on 'possessions and poverty' and 'social justice', we can say in conclusion that Jesus' teaching offered (good news of) substantial and structural liberation and justice to the poor, deprived and oppressed. And we can say that Jesus' teaching was good and happy news in the ears of the poor, deprived and oppressed in a way that our witness and praxis as Church has not always been good news to them today. It is worth remarking that Jesus' blessing went to the poor not primarily because they were subjectively '*good*', '*simple*' or '*holy*' or had any other moral qualification. Biblical concern goes out to the poor primarily *because they were poor*. The focus of Jesus' remarks (cf., Luke 16:19–31; Luke 6:20; Mark 10:21, etc.) was not so much the goodness of the poor as the *poverty of the poor*.

(e) What about the rich?

And what was Jesus' view of the rich or the non-poor? How did he relate to them? The rich in Jesus' life seem to be one of the following: those criticised by Jesus (e.g., 'Woe to you rich' Luke 6:24); those challenged by Jesus (e.g., the rich young man who was asked by Jesus to sell his possessions and give to the poor: Mark 10:21); those who were converted and shared their riches (e.g., Zacchaeus, Luke 19:1–10) or those who had faith in Jesus (and presumably, in everything Jesus stood for, including justice and liberation for the poor), and not an oppressor (e.g., the women who followed Jesus, Luke 8:2; the Roman centurion, Luke 7;1–10).

But, did Jesus not die for rich and poor alike? Yes, he eventually died for rich and poor. But, while he was living, he stood for justice and liberation for the poor. And this stance for the poor in all likelihood had something to do with his death at the hands of the powerful and wealthy of his time.

But, did not Jesus proclaim the good news of the kingdom to all—rich and poor alike? Yes, he did. The invitation to the kingdom is for all. But because of the demands of the kingdom, it was often bad news for the wealthy and powerful (e.g., Mark 10:21–22; Luke 14:15–24).

Since Jesus died for rich and poor, should not the Church today also minister to the rich? Yes: The only question is *how*? It is not enough that the rich appropriate the spiritual grace of Jesus' death in baptism and nurture it in the sacraments. The rich must also be asked to live according to the kingdom demands of Jesus.

6. A QUESTION FOR THE CHRISTIAN CONSCIENCE

In five hundred years of Catholic and Reformation theology, we have listed the deeds of Jesus before, during and after his earthly life except his proclamation of liberation and justice to the poor (good news to the poor). And yet, it is mentioned in the principal mission statements; it is the *only act*[3] of Jesus that is *constantly* mentioned in *different* mission statements; it is, therefore, embedded at the very heart of Jesus' mission! A question for the Christian conscience is: Why then has the Gospel of liberation and justice for the poor not been part of the Christian conscience for several hundred years? It is today's poor and their struggle that have challenged us to go back to our biblical roots and rediscover the Gospel of justice and liberation in the very core of Jesus' original mission. May this Gospel in turn help to fire us to dedicate ourselves to the task of justice and liberation in our time.

Notes

1. For example, Isaiah 52:7–10; 35:1–10; 29:17–21; 61:1–4.
2. For example, Mark 2:5.
3. The other act often mentioned is 'giving sight to the blind'.

Norbert Brox

'Making Earth into Heaven': Diakonia in the Early Church

DIAKONIA IS frequently discussed with great seriousness in early Church sources. It formed as much a part of the consciousness of the early Church as preaching the Gospel. It would be even better to say that it was regarded as one of the ways of proclaiming the truth of Jesus of Nazareth. If Christians were present where there was human need, as a community actively helping, healing and bringing about changes, this had the effect of a sermon without words—or instead of words (see 1 Pet. 3:1f.). Like the sermon on the Cross, the ministry of helping one's neighbour—going beyond the necessity of social aid—was experienced as bearing witness to faith. This activity was remarked by non-Christian contemporaries, firstly as something unusual and striking and then, at least partly, as something that could convince and point the way. For Christians, diakonia was a reality in which the redemption that they preached could already begin before death in this life, by transforming poverty, distress, sadness and death through the power of love. The Church Fathers expressed this in symbols and theological ideas, a few of which will be discussed in this article. And, since the Church cannot be dispensed from its need to carry out this ministry, the diakonia can never be a purely arbitrary matter that is simply left to chance. I hope to show in this article that the early Church took great care to see that there was always a diakonia.

1. 'SEE HOW THEY LOVE ONE ANOTHER'

Tertullian, who liked to write about the pagans' reaction to Christians and about the striking ways in which Christians differed from others in public life at the time, must have heard these words spoken by non-Christians quite often. They were, however, even household words (see *Apol.* 39,7). What, then, was it that surprised non-Christians so much about Christians? Tertullian tells us himself—they spent their money supporting and burying poor people, helping those orphans who had no other support and 'pensioners' without a pension, paying for those whom misfortune had brought into distress and for those who were banished or in prison. There was no such social initiative or love of one's neighbour that had been made obligatory by religion or morality in the later ancient world. There was a kind of private generosity and beneficence at that time, but any attempt that was made to establish real care and justice was aimed only at 'decent' people. Christians, on the other hand, insisted on the fundamentally obligatory nature of what they carried out as diakonia or service of their fellow-men. They made no conditions. It is sufficient to document this with textual examples, since such texts would not have existed if they had not been covered by the reality itself.

The social practices of this new kind of religious group, the Christians, were, then, according to Tertullian and others, very striking. They themselves wanted them to be striking and they liked speaking about them, quite often in the context of the Sermon on the Mount. According to the Greek Christian Athenagoras, for example, writing in the second century (*Suppl.* 11): 'Among us you can find uneducated people, craftsmen and old women, who cannot discuss the usefulness of (Christian) teaching in words, but who can prove the usefulness of their decision by their activity. They are not constantly using words, but are exhibiting good deeds. When they are struck, they do not hit back and when they are robbed, they do not go to court. They give to those who ask them and they love their fellow-men as themselves'.

Christianity, then, is in a very authentic way also mediated and made a reality non-verbally, that is, through the medium of such selfless activity and such a selfless attitude. At the end of the second century, Minucius Felix could write (*Oct.* 38,6): 'We do not speak of good things. We do them'. And the poor, the sick and the injured, the widows and orphans and others are mentioned again and again as recipients of this care (*Pol Phil.* 6,1) as well as the strangers and the dead (for burial) and the persecuted and the prisoners (Aristides, *Apol.* 15,4–9; Lactantius, *Div. Inst.* 6,11. 6–12.31). Support can also be gained by the fact that this way of behaving has no intention: 'The good works that they do are not proclaimed aloud into the ears of many people. They take care that they are not noticed' (Artistides, *Apol.* 16,2). It is in *being carried out* that the diakonia has meaning and at the same time gains support.

This diakonia, then, was an everyday affair. In situations of extreme crisis, Christians stood out even more prominently from their environment, in which comparable duties did not exist, by simply continuing to carry out their duty. A vivid example of this is provided by Eusebius in his report of a catastrophic case of plague and starvation during the reign of Emperor Maximinus at the beginning of the fourth century. We should perhaps disregard a certain exaggeration of Christian virtue on the part of the author, but the text does show us what was required among Christians and what they in fact gave at the time. He writes (*Hist. Eccl.* 8,13f.): 'The all-embracing and serious zeal and the piety of Christians was demonstrated then in clear signs to all pagans. For they were the only ones who, in such a catastrophe, provided evidence, by their immediate intervention, of their sympathy and their love for their fellow-men. Some were ceaselessly active the whole day long in their care of the dying and their interment—there were thousands for whom not a single person cared. Others took the many people who were suffering terribly from hunger out of the great city, brought them together in one place and distributed bread to all of them. What they did was talked about by everyone . People praised the God of Christians and recognised that only they were the truly pious and God-fearing men, since their activity proved it'.

What the diakonia consisted of, both in everyday and in extraordinary situations, should be clear from these examples. There was a widespread conviction that Christianity could be recognised by its concrete forms. And Christian who belonged to the early Church were also not mistaken in their belief that this was both striking and contagious. There are also pagan texts giving evidence of this, some mocking (much of it, like that written by Lucian in the second century, not very ingenious) and others showing that the authors were impressed.

The most spectacular example is the reaction of the non-Christian Emperor Julian (361–363), called by Christians the Apostate. He had been opposed to Christianity from his youth onwards, but he was familiar with the Church's care of the poor and general diakonia. What he had come to know as a child broughout up with a Christian education he tried as emperor to mediate to his people through his pagan priests. What he expressed as his aim was the introduction of the Christian praxis of the ministry of love (although admittedly without Christianity). He carried that out consciously, calling on his people to compete with the Christians: 'We must take care! What godlessness (that is, Christanity) has promoted most of all is human friendliness towards strangers, care for the interment of the dead and apparent purity in one's way of life. Each of these virtues must, I think, be exercised by us with sincere zeal' (*Ep.* 39, Weis).

Although it was not his intention, Julian's polemics against Christianity become a corroboration. According to him, the old Roman religion should be restored in praxis by imitating the Christian diakonia and he consequently called on his priests to help the poor—including the poor of the enemy—to care for prisoners and to exercise hospitality. These were all areas covered by the Christian diakonia (*Ep.* 48, Weis). He could not resort to the pagan tradition for this service and had to make a caricature of Christian examples (see, for instance, *Ep.* 48,305C, Weis) so that they should not be recognised. It should be clear from this, then, how regular, striking and impressive the diakonia of the early Church was in public life in the fourth century. It also drew attention to the deficiency in the value-concepts of non-Christian society, which had no comparable diakonia. According to Julian (*Ep.* 305BC, Weis), 'it is to this point particularly (human love) that attention has to be given and a cure has to be found. It has, I believe, reached the stage where the poor have been overlooked and neglected by our priests, with the result that the godless Galilaeans (that is, the Christians), having noticed this, have applied themselves to this practice of love of their fellow-men ... In this way, child thieves are exchanging their sacrifice for a cake ...' The productive and contagious effect of the very different social behaviour of early Christians practising diakonia can be recognised in this calumny.

2. MAKING EARTH INTO HEAVEN

John Chrysostom (d. 407) went much further as a presbyter and a bishop in a large city than others with the social question and the Church's obligation to deal with its consequences, even evolving, for example, a vision of a redistribution of all the possessions of Christians so that there would be no more poor people. He thought the entire question through to the point of developing realiable alternatives based on love in a Christianised society. It was in this context that he made use of the audacious metaphor of 'heaven on earth': 'God said: "I have made earth and heaven. I give you too creative power. Make earth into heaven! You can do this!" ' (In *Ep. I ad Tim. Hom.* 15,4; *PG* 62,585f.). And that in fact happens in the new life of Christians—the life of the Church; there 'we make earth into heaven' (In *Mt. Hom.* 43 al. 44,5; *PG* 57.463).

This is, of course, the language of Utopia, but John had an image of it that could be realised or in any case thought of and would become a reality if only Christians were able to understand and commit themselves to radical love and the Church were able to understand and commit itself to a consistent diakonia. In the question of rich and poor, for example, it was possible to calculate that the sale of everyone's land, buildings and posessions would raise enough to guarantee the care of the fifty thousand poor in Constantinople. John uses his Utopian idea to comment: 'Would we not (in this way) make earth into heaven?' (In *Acta Apost. Hom.* 11,3; *PG* 60,98). He saw this diakonia or living for others as something that could transform the earth—as salvation that had already dawned and no simply as a sign for it, although admittedly it was not the entire promise of the Gospel. It is clear, then, that John placed a very high value on the Church's praxis of diakonia.

It is quite consistent with this that he also made it a criterion for the Church and for Christian life, a criterion that he placed alongside that of orthodoxy. The realisation of God's plan consisted of diakonia and orthodoxy together. 'God is glorified not only by right doctrines', he wrote (In *Gen. Sermo* 1,3; *PG* 54,585), 'but also by the best possible (Christian) way of life'. And elsewhere (In *Joh. Hom.* 67 al. 66,3; *PG* 59,374), he also wrote: 'not only by faith, but also by life'.

One is reminded here of Bishop Firmilianus of Caesarea in Asian Minor, who, in the better debate about the baptism of heretics that took place in the middle of the third century, insisted on the validity of the 'rule of truth *and* peace' (see Cyprian, *Ep.* 75,24), in other words, on the unity and foundation of the Church in orthodoxy *and* in the praxis of what was essentially Christian (in this instance, peace).

This balance in the concept of the Church was to a great extent lost, at least in its early Christian explicit form, as Christianity became increasingly doctrinalised in the course of the fourth and fifth centuries.

Two things had still to be said to the recipient of the community's diakonia. Gal. 6:10 was, as it were, the official text of the earlier situation, stating that the community's service applied to all persons, but was in fact concentrated predominantly on Christians, in other words, on solidarity within the Church. The social isolation of Christians especially in pre-Constantinian times and the limited means that were available then must also have played an important part in this. There were, however, always exceptions, especially in cases of catastrophe (see below) and, during the period of the imperial Church, the situation was quite different, as the Church was also materially supported by the state. Even among Christians, however, aid was not given without a process of selection. The basis and the degree of the need had to be assessed and the age and status of the persons had to be borne in mind (see Origen, *Co. Ser. in Mt.* 61; *GCS* 34,142; cf. *Did.* 12,1). Valerian of Cemele (d. ca. 460) expressed quite a different view: 'Why do you trouble yourself with the question as to whether the one seeking help is a Christian or a Jew, a heretic or a pagan, a Roman or a barbarian, a freeman or a slave? Where there is need, the question of the person in need does not have to be discussed. That you may not—by excluding certain persons as unworthy of merciful help—at the same time send away the Son of God!'

In this question, at least according to the decision made by Basil of Caesarea

(d. 379; *Hom*. 1,6 in *Ps* 14; *PG* 29,261C), only both Origen and Valerian together would seem to be right: ' "Give to him who begs from you" (Matt. 5:42). These words mean that you should be, towards those who beg from you, on the one hand completely generous, and without suspicion and out of love, but, on the other hand, that you should sensibly ascertain the need of everyone who begs from you'. In principle, this diakonia has no limits.

3. THE ORGANISATION OF THE DIAKONIA

The early Church, then, institutionalised its ministry in order to exercise it constantly and not to forget it. There was unlimited care for a number of widows chosen from the community on the basis of certain criteria. This care of widows (not only widowed women) is an early form of this ministry (see 1 Tim. 5:3–16; Ign. *Sm*. 6,2; Pol. *Phil*. 4,3). These women were also seen as having a special 'status' and were given particular functions in the community. From the middle of the second century (see Justin, *Apol*. 1,67), Sunday collections were set aside as a precondition for helping the poor. The importance of the diakonia is also clear from the fact that the means for it were managed by the bishop—in other words, he was in charge of the treasury and the places where the food was stored. In addition to regular collections, there were also special donations and the savings made on fast days, all of which produced the necessary means. In this way, all Christians, including those who had no means at all, were able to share in the diakonia that was constantly and publicly managed by the bishop.

Under the conditions of the imperial Church, this diakonia became a form of social aid with a similar form of administration. The bishops continued to exercise their power to dispose of the often very considerable means and even extended the organisation of the services. Because of this, it was possible, for example, for Basil to construct a settlement where the sick, the poor and the strangers could be accommodated and to organise work there (see Gregory of Nazianzen, *Orat*. 43,63; Basil, *Ep*. 94,142–144; cf. *Did*. 12,4). There were also other hospices and hospitals, mostly financed by donations, and the part played by the monastic orders in the Church's social work from the fourth century onwards is well known.

4. 'CHRIST IN THE POOR'

The diakonia administered to those in need was not a profane activity. The Church encounted Christ in the poor. This presence of Christ can easily be misrepresented and the resulting service of Christ correspondingly neglected. Gregory of Nyssa (*Orat*. I, ed. A. van Heck, Leiden, 1964; 8,23–9,2) warned: 'Do not despise the humiliated, as though they had no dignity. Remember who they are and then you will find their dignity: They have assumed the appearance of our redeemer. For he has, in his love for men, bestowed his own appearance on them, so that they might in this way put to shame those (A. van Heck has a different reading here, 81: *Adducant ad misericordiam, concilient*) who are without sympathy and who do not care for the poor'.

Where, then, is Matt. 25:35–46 given concrete expression in the writings of the early Fathers? Gregory expresses it succinctly: 'He (that is, Christ) is for you a stranger, naked, in need of food, sick, in prison and everything that is predicted in the Gospel. He goes around without a home, naked, sick and lacking the most necessary things'. The Church Fathers speak of the poor as the 'place' of Christ's presence here and now and use this to explain the diakonia or service of the poor as a service of Christ. Gregory of Nazianzen, for example (*Orat*. 14,40; *PG* 35,909), declared: 'As long as there is still time, we want to visit Christ, care for Christ, feed Christ, clothe Christ, gather up Christ, value Christ ... Since the All Powerful wants mercy and not sacrifices (Hos. 6:6; Matt. 9:13) and mercy is more valuable than thousands of fat lambs (Dan. 3:40), we are to take these things to him in the poor and in those who have been thrown today to the ground'. In a word, Christ is 'there' in the poor (see Salvian, *Eccl*. 4,4; Jerome, *Ep*. 130,14).

Diakonia, then, is serving Christ, who is himself directly in need of help of the poor. According to Jerome, 'Christ is clothed in the poor, visited in the sick, fed in the hungry and given shelter in those who have no roof over their head' (*Ep*. 130,14). In the fifth century, Salvian of Merseilles expressed this idea in the following way: All the individual suffering of many people is gathered together in Christ and Christ bears all suffering at the same time; the whole pressure of suffering of the world is Christ's passion and Christ is the sum total of all the poor (*Eccl*. 2,4.7; 4,4). He was so convinced of this that he, a presbyter, went to a rich Christian in a high position to persuade him—unsuccessfully—not to make a poor devil who was his debtor even poorer (*Gub*. 4,15). He regarded this form of help of the poor as his diakonia, his way of serving those suffering distress. He was also deeply disappointed by the failure of priests and bishops to intervene on his behalf of the poor and protested: 'Who will let help be given to those who are tormented and suffer, since not even priests of the Lord of power will oppose wicked men (= rich men and authorities)? Most of them are silent or it makes no difference even if they speak ... because they will not express the obvious truth, since the ears of the wicked men cannot bear it ... and that is why they are silent, though they could speak' (*Gub*. 5,5). In exactly the same way, Salvian also criticised the unjust and brutal practice of raising taxes and disappropriating land, the asocial bestowing of favours on the rich, the over-lapping of interests between the clergy and those who owned property (*Gub.* 5,5) and the immoderate extent of meaningless public expenditure that did not help the poor in any way.

The Christian duty and necessity of diakonia, then, can also be illustrated from the perspective of the Church's failure to provide it, as Salvian did in the apparently hopeless situation of his own times. Like other clearsighted Christians living in the first centuries, he struggled, despite his experience to the contrary. For the Church (at that time at Gaul and Aquitania) to be concerned with the poor and the diakonia, so that, in the words of John Chrysostom, 'earth' might be made 'into heaven', because being a Christian meant 'uniting oneself with man' (Lactantius, *Div. Inst.* 6,10,2). The image of heaven on earth can also be expressed in another way, namely that diakonia tries to end the hell that the earth is for many people.[1]

Translated by David Smith

Notes

1. I will mention only three of the many books on this subject: S. Giet *Les idées et l'action sociales de saint Basile* (Paris 1941); R. Brändtle *Matt. 25,31–46 im Werk des Johannes Chrysostomos* (Tübingen 1979); W.-d. Hauschild 'Armenfürsorge II. Alte Kirche', *TRE* IV, 1979, pp. 14–23.

Ottmar Fuchs

Church for Others

'The Church is only the Church
when it is there for other people' (D. Bonhoeffer)

The Church's Identity through Service

1. AN INTRODUCTION TO THE THESIS

BONHOEFFER'S ASSERTION sounds resolute and provocative,
especially if we think what its negation would be: the Church is not the Church
if it is not there for other people, if—we might go on to say—it is there only for
its own sake, merely as an in-group of believers with the appropriate
ideological self-certainties and institutional structures, which then determine
the character of the Church's social forms. 'Existence for other people' is
different. It definitely (also) means the people who really are 'the others'—all
the people who do not belong to the Church, as an institutional and doctrinal
community of faith. It means especially the people who—according to the
faith and morals which the Church approves—count as unbelievers, sinners,
outsiders, aliens. The Church is there so as to be there for these 'others': so as
to expand the opportunities of living open to them and the quality of their
lives. And it has to do this through direct, helping amd liberating encounters
and groups, as well as by way of humane social structures and just economic
conditions.

This is the Church's task, formulated in general terms. But it catches fire in
the real and specific places where these 'others' are suffering, the places where
they are living in poverty and need, despised and oppressed, in unjust
conditions, or where their very lives are threatened. These 'ignition points' are

not matters of choice. They are the places where the ministries of the Church are necessarily expended. The Church, that is to say, is only the Church when it helps those who need help, and helps the helpers to help, and when it liberates the oppressed and helps the liberators in their task of liberation: and all this irrespective of who these 'others' are. This is the praxis in which the Church is auuthentically the Church, because its identity comes into being through service.

For the well-disposed, this perhaps sounds so obvious that its explosive quality, as criticism of the Church, may not at first appear, or be grasped. Yet here nothing less than the Church's identity *per se* is in question. For here service for others is made the decisive criterion for distinguishing in the Church's praxis between its maintaining of itself as institution and its solidarity with others; between faith and ideology; between love and rule; between liberation and domination; between Baal and Yahweh—ultimately between godlessness and trust in God, or between anti-Christian conduct and discipleship. We sense especially that this touches the very nerve-centre of the Church's self-developed structures when we observe the history-long ambivalence of its defence of the faith and its defence of its own institutions, seeing these things critically against the background of unconditional service—which means service hindered by no inhibiting conditions.

2. NEIGHBOURLY LOVE IN THE CHURCH AND ITS LIMITATIONS: CREDIT AND DEBIT

As the Christian churches grew up, it was their inestimable achievement, on the basis of a new religious unity, to cross frontiers in their own social spheres. These frontiers had hitherto seldom been infringed; and some of them— religious, ethical, political and socio-cultural—were heavily charged with restrictive sanctions. Yet, as the Church increasingly constituted itself as group and formed its identity, it inevitably created new dividing lines between what were now Christian congregations and their non-Christian environment. Here the development of the concepts 'heathen' and 'heresy' is significant.[1] There are certainly already movements running counter to this trend in the New Testament writings, and among early Christian theologians—writers who stress love of one's enemies, or unconditional service for all who suffer.[2] Yet we can detect an apparently ever-more dominant narrowing down of the universal character of *neighbourly* love to that of *brotherly* love within the Church.[3] Service for others finds its scope mainly within the limits of the new communities.

Of course there is nothing to be said against mutual service in and among Christian congregations. Only it is then easy to lose sight of the fact that there are people outside the Church who are not only in need of redeeming faith, but who also require help in their distress, and liberation from oppression. This aspect of the Jesus of Nazareth about whom the Gospels tell, recedes into the background, while doctrinaire apologetic and institutional demarcation lines between Christians and heathen, or between Christians and Jews, push themselves all the more to the fore.

In the first three centuries the minority status of the Christian congregations, and the occasional oppression they suffered, may serve as excuse for this development. But after the change of conditions under Constantine, this no longer applies. The Church was now on the way to becoming a majority with a share in state power; and it was precisely as its influence increased that the frontiers between Christians and heathen were drawn more strictly, against the background of the new conditions of power. As a result, non-Christians increasingly experienced their dissident status in the form of defamation, discrimination and maltreatment.[4] Christians and Church ceased to be aware, spiritually, theologically and ecclesiologically, that this kind of conduct towards 'unbelievers' was a slap in the face for the universal ministry, depriving the transmission of faith of its essential communicative basis, replacing it by an improper (because unchristian) more or less forced indoctrination and a press-gang type of integration. From here, not much stands in the way of developments in the Church's history leading to the 'wars of religion', pogroms and 'Christian' colonisations.

Here a contemptuous totalitarian ideology stands unspoken sponsor: unbelievers do not deserve humane treatment—or deserve it less than believers. Consequently it is easier to accept the sufferings of non-believers than the bitter experiences of Christians. More: it is even legitimate to increase the sufferings of unbelievers, through pain and oppression, since they really deserve nothing else, or in order to bring them at last to true faith. To put it in somewhat vulgar terms: people may surely be forced for their own good 'to get to heaven'. The unbeliever can easily avoid suffering of this kind if he will only let himself be told what the truth is, and enter the fold of the Church.

The ministering love of the Christian God is radical in its universality. It is wide open. This God loves human beings as sinners without any conditions, and desires their salvation even before they change their ways (cf., Rom. 5:8 and John 4:10). But this love is obscured if the ministering love of Christians is dependent on the condition that the sinner must first of all enter the institutional and ideological fold of the Church, and adopt the good behaviour bound up with that. Christians and the Church would, rather, be preaching the Gospel to themselves if they spelled out the 'limits' of their faith by *tearing down* the limits on loving service for all. The persecuted Jews and the Communist in the concentration camp, the AIDS-infected homosexual and the slandered man or woman seeking political asylum—all these people belong to the social domain of the Christian Church and its charitable service, and to the sphere of its solidarity, simply because they claim help and need liberation. This prevents the mentality which is seriously prepared to help only if certain moral, ideological or institutional conditions are fulfilled.

3. THE FRUITFUL TENSION BETWEEN KOINONIA (FELLOWSHIP) AND DIAKONIA (SERVICE)

If we see the problem in this light, then the concept of 'brotherly love' is surely insufficient to cover a 'Church for others'. It may also be too undifferentiated, since it does not distinguish clearly enough between *koinonia* (the fellowship of believers) and *diakonia* (service to the suffering, including strangers and opponents, which continually tears down the barriers of the 'internal' fellowship). Moreover, brotherly love all too easily suggests that service for others is exhausted in service for 'the brethren'.[5] But in fact the Church's two dimensions stand in considerable tension to one another, in terms both of social psychology and institutional theory; for no interest group willingly puts someone at the centre who does not 'belong', or hold the same opinions.

This tension will not emerge, however, if service is made over to a separate church organisation, as in the Catholic church in West Germany, with its Caritasverband. The parishes then feel that they have been relieved of this task. If we look at the resulting practice, in the Church's *koinonia* (fellowship) and *diakonia* (service for others), we see that there really is unconditional ministry for *all* the suffering and oppressed; but this is confined largely to the initiatives and institutions of the Caritas association. Caritas has 28,000 instittions (hospitals, homes for the handicapped, social and counselling centres, etc.) and 300,000 full time workers, thereby being the largest charitable organisation in West Germany.[6] But these initiatives and institutions are relatively cut off from the parishes. Consequently the parishes could and can without embarrassment concentrate on 'more essential' sectors of passing on the faith, through proclamation in word and sacrament. So in over 50 per cent of West German parishes, service for others plays a highly reduced role, generally as a particular topic on special collection Sundays.[7] The other 50 per cent (especially the student congregations) are increasingly and unerringly sensitive to, and aware of, local needs. They concern themselves with the possible organisation of help and with supra-regional solidarity actions. Though here, certainly, local parishes should watch more carefully to see how far service is limited to Catholics. For example, does a

Catholic kindergarten accept Turkish children [i.e., the children of immigrant Turkish workers]?

This state of affairs cannot be considered satisfactory. The practice of the parishes is often considered legitimate, because the Caritas organisation exists. But if the parishes make themselves primarily places for liturgical celebration and confessional ideology in the sphere of an ecclesiastically accepted religiosity and morality, they then delegate the concerns of charitable service (if they even know what these concerns are) to some other authority, away from the congregation; and this authority 'represents' the congregation to all those in need. The parish certainly pays highly for this delegation in financial terms. But it is saved *direct encounter* with those affected.[8]

This 'organising away' of people who are in need and on the fringes of society has catastrophic effects for the build-up of the congregation itself, as well as for the needy, the oppressed and underprivileged, in the area served by a given parish. For the problem of professional charity is that it easily estimates—and underestimates—as dilettante, any non-professional, spontaneous, simple, everyday, matter of course, effective ways of helping by 'lay' people, or their ability for service.[9] Yet without the 'infrastructure' of minds orientated towards ministry, and the corresponding communicative reality of a wider social network, the highly cultivated professionalism of the charitable organisation is left in the air of specialist care and treatment, which is insufficiently carried over and continued in ordinary everyday life.

For example, the hospital treatment offered by state and charitable organisations is highly necessary, especially for those suffering from AIDS in its acute stages; yet it proves relatively helpless when it comes down to the social contexts to which people with AIDS return, in their often relatively long symptom-free periods—whether they can live there in dignity (i.e., accepted and perceived as important for others), and whether they can discuss their situation, master it or endure it. The best counselling or care remains an unrelated experience unless there are also special, alternative social forms on an intermediary level (between family and the major social structures) in which those affected are not exposed to social discrimination but are given jobs, support and places to live. And the local churches would belong precisely to this 'between' level.

Moreover only the lived sensibility for service of Christians and congregations can probably perceive the need which lives beyond the zones of need defined by the charitable organisations, and outside the receiver-range accepted by the financial bureaucracy.[10] The problems 'the welfare state' has about accepting 'the new poverty' in Germany (but not only there) belongs here; though the real experience of the people concerned make this poverty undeniable.

Because there is so little social contact with the handicapped, the distressed, and those suffering from discrimination, we lose the particular 'competences' which these people have to offer and can claim, for a perception of what the Gospel means and for the beginnings of a practical realisation of the kingdom of God. Practised ministry always changes the witness itself, which is to say the proclamation of the Gospel; for learning how to think and live from people who are suffering means that the practice of faith is changed and radicalised, in the context of options that are no longer optional but quite literally necessary—born of need. The suffering do not merely have a claim to help; they always have something important to say as well. That is surely why Jesus does not merely put a child in the midst, as the object of helpful service (because 'not yet being grown up' counts as a deficiency); he makes children the actual yardstick for 'grown ups' in their dealings with the kingdom of God (Matt. 19:13–14).

Here we can discover possible ways of learning, ways we can hope for, particularly in encounters with the suffering; for the helpers help those who need it *and*, anticipating that the suffering can help them, accept help in their turn. This help takes the form of disquieting yet ultimately salutary questions put to their own forms of living, their attitudes, their suppression of weakness and powerlessness, their perhaps pathologising and alienating forms of behaviour, structures and ideologies. The person who suffers always has an essentially critical, transforming and intensifying quality for all concerned.

What is in question here, therefore, is not a new moralisation of service. It simply means being encouraged to expect and accept, even in such encounters—and there especially—a decisive message about more humane living. 'The complementary community' comes about only in the mutual fellowship of helpers and those who need help, the healthy and the sick, the strong and the weak, where roles can be exchanged and where their possibilities and impossibilities do not have to be either left unexploited or suppressed, but can be 'lumped together' to provide the great opportunity for a more humane church.[11]

4. THE SCOPE OF SERVICE IN THE COMMUNITY OF THE CHURCH AND IN PASTORAL CARE

Service for others provokes the breaking down of barriers in two directions, permanently stripping faith of its ideological character, and dissolving institutional restrictions. Barriers *inwards* are broken down, because people who are in need belong from the outset to the centre of the Church and to its special sphere of responsibility, simply *because* they are in need (not, for example, because they 'belong'). Barriers *outwards* are destroyed when Christians and church work together with all initiatives and groups, and with all men and women of good will, showing solidarity with those who—in their actions and in their siding with those who suffer, at home and abroad—aim to expose and combat social-political and economic causes of distress.

This dynamic, truly communicative exchange process between Church and society in the ministry which bridges the two, is the mark showing that Christians and Church manifest their identity *through* service. The universality of service to people inside and outside, in and between Church and society, is the historical and the specific, situational expression of the Church's character as universal sacrament for the world. This universality of salvation in ministry as a whole means the criticism of all manifestations of the Church which, content with their own dynamic (and understandably enough, psychologically) try to fence themselves off, and if necessary to exclude 'outsiders'. This is so especially in the spheres where people meet in liturgy and worship, or where faith seeks to assure itself of its doctrinal truth or moral standards.

Accordingly, while claiming unlimited scope outwards, wherever there is distress, *diakonia*—ministry—claims the same scope inwardly too, in a special sense: that is, within the community (*koinonia*) of the Church's own social forms. To deny divorced and remarried people admission to the sacraments is in this light behaviour hostile to ministry in the liturgical sphere (or in the conditions for admission to the sacraments laid down by canon law). Equally hostile to ministry is the longstanding contemptuous treatment of applications for laicisation made by priests (treatment in the interests of a law that is in any case theologically questionable). The result here is unnecessary conflict and oppressive inhumanity. And when the Congregation for the Doctrine of the Faith, writing about the pastoral care of homosexuals,[12] denies them the title of 'believers in Christ' (which is always otherwise applied in such texts to baptised and confirmed Christians), then a verdict prompted by sexual morality is standing in the way of humane dealings with people belonging to a fringe group. Strictly moral Catholics then do not offer these people the congregation's help, even for the sake of ministering to AIDS-infected or AIDS sufferers.

In view of what I have merely touched on here, I am unable to accept the assertion that the unlimited scope of ministry 'has, for example, no direct consequences for admission to the Eucharist'.[13] Here a dubious distinction is made between ministry and liturgy which cannot be legitimated by Jesus' own behaviour; for his Last Supper was the ultimate expression and final seal of all the previous meals he shared with sinners and those on the fringes of society, and the seal too of the ministry of them he thereby lived. This cannot be separated from the sacrament of the Eucharist, any more than the Jesus we hear about in the gospels can be separated from the Christ of faith. It is for me too litle, and also considerably too wayward, to talk merely about 'an analogous relationship of interdependence between charitable service and Eucharist'.[14] In the context of christological paradigmatics, we have rather to talk about a perichoresis—an unmingled intertwining of Eucharist and *diakonia*, the real presence of Christ in the sacrament and his real presence through the ministry of love in the community of Christians, and hence through the Church.[15] For the risen one himself appears in strangers and the sick (cf., Matt. 25:35–36), just as he is also really present, through his Spirit, in all those who help and liberate.

This interactive Christo-praxis between helpers and sufferers, the rejected and those who receive them, gives Christology in the sphere of faith and Christodoxology in the sphere of worship their all-embracing dimension—the dimension comprehending the whole of life. Faith and worship then no longer act as a blockade against unrestricted service. They are experienced as the enabling foundation and context of a ministry which devotes itself without ifs and buts to the underprivileged, the sick and those in need. People who believe that their whole existence is hid with God until death and beyond, *can*—out of this inexhaustible fact of God's love—give themselves to suffering men and women. Since God's love is already theirs without reserve, they can give unreserved love themselves, and spend themselves within the limits of their possiblities and the impotence they experience.

The saving universality of the Eucharist, and hence its 'ministering' dimension, should therefore be maintained, at least for all baptised Christians,[16] so that in the Church people may discover that, in its own sphere, the Church deals with sinners (or those whom it deems sinners) in exactly the same way that God, in his infinite readiness for reconciliation, encounters sinners: that is, in unconditional love—not merely after they have duly changed their ways, but beforehand, so that they *can* change, within the framework of their own possibilities. God's righteousness does not set up any meritocratic conditions. He justifies sinners and the godless. All Christians have a right to a praxis of ministry in everything that happens in the Church— a praxis in which grace goes before law, and where love is freed from the position of morality.[17]

The different conditions in which Christians live are always fragmentary. One person lives more in the sphere of explicit faith, another more in the sphere of charitable service, again others rather in the common life of the Christian community. It is only on the basis of mutual service, and in the acceptance of mutual limitations, that Christians can take one another seriously, and all the more so by exposing themselves to mutual criticism. The more the dimension of service is committed to be directly effective in all spheres of the Church's own life and social forms, the more the Church will itself internally become the social field *where service is learnt*; and it can then offer this service 'outwards, to everyone, all the more effectively, and with all the more experience. In this way *koinonia* (community) becomes the foundation for the universal *diakonia* (service) of Christians and the Church towards all human beings. It becomes the place where its own necessity and the necessity of others is discovered. But it is the place too for discussing helpful and liberating acts for those who need help, and for the helpers. So unless the Church's pastoral ministry is service 'inwards'—communicating the gracious God *there*, in the Church itself—it will hardly be able to provide the corresponding basic experience which is required for its ministry 'outwards'.

5. THE PRIORITY OF SERVICE AS PRINCIPLE

In all cases, and in principle, service is the essential option which determines the ordering of all other priorities. This must be the fundamental policy or programme, as long as there are people who suffer in the area to which a congregation belongs, or in its sphere of experience, or in the remoter sectors about which it hears. It is therefore not merely a question of the 'situational priority' of service 'under particular conditions of congregational life',[15] because Christians and congregations *are*, in principle and from the outset, 'the neighbour' of people in need; and they have to seek these people out, and discover where they are (Luke 10:36). It is not for the person in need to force himself on the congregation's attention first of all, proving that he is their neighbour. They have to discover *him*, since they have made the fundamental existential decision that they will be the neighbours of the suffering. One cannot invest all one's energy in something or other—even if it is by no means bad in itself (liturgy and catechesis, for example)—if, close by, AIDS victims are dying a social death, and are hence not infrequently in danger of suicide. Service is not an optional subject in pastoral care. It is essential. This means that *diakonia* is not at the option of the person who has to decide, but is dependent on the really existing need itself.

But of course if people do not make *diakonia*, or service, a principle, but speak only of 'situational priority', this will easily impair the ability to perceive need and oppression, even where the sufferers do not make themselves known, or are prevented by strategies of appeasement from crying their need aloud. Moreover it is only the fundamental priority of *diakonia* which will make people unerringly watchful to discern need; though here the background must be the also fundamental premise that suffering people themselves have the authority to define their situation and to plead their own cause. Recognition of this principle differentiates the explosive power of the concept of evangelisation and the praxis or theology of liberation from all other theological outlines.[19] Only people who from the outset accept the priority of the suffering in their theology and spirituality will be able to perceive a specific 'situational priority' at all; and they will avoid making the discernment of need and the discussion about active help depend (solely) on what they or others think best (unless they are the sufferers themselves, or have to do with them).

If we ask what ought to have a permanent 'systematic' priority, before the merely situational priority of service, then of course we arrive at the answer: the proclamation of the Gospel, and worship. Yet if we look at the Jesus Christ of whom the gospels tell, we have surely to perceive that what he says about the kingdom of God and about God himself is said pre-eminently in the context of encounters in which he has already acted, as healer; or where he has entered into dispute on behalf of the poor and despised. So recourse to this origin forces us to accept that in principle talk about God is not talk about God at all without the praxis of active ministry (*diakonia*) and that the praxis of ministry is always the point at which we can and must talk about God.

This is very important, because one does not have to be explicitly affected by the Gospel before one is able to discover the needs of other people (in the interests of the Gospel too).[20] If this were not so we should have to put down any solidarity and discernment of need that is not motivated by Christianity and the Church as 'optional social work' and depreciate it as something that has nothing to do with God. Certainly, many Christians acquire greater sensibility towards the perception of suffering because they have been touched by the Gospel. But on the other hand, human need touches the love and compassion of many people directly, as we are told it touched Jesus. They practise the Gospel in the world, even though the Gospel is never mentioned.[21]

For centuries the Gospel was read by most interpreters of the Church without their being touched at all in the way we have described. Much suggests that it is only the perception of distress which provides the material hermeneutics[22] for reading the Gospel in such a way that it has to do with the real hope: that there is a point in combatting necessity and oppression in the light of the kingdom of God, because the kingdom thereby acquires reality, in germ, in the way men and women shape their lives. And it is this reality alone which has a future, down to the coming of that kingdom and into the kingdom itself. Accordingly it is true to say that people who allow themselves to be touched by the need of others will never read the Gospel except with the eyes of compassion, and will discover the corresponding faith. This will be so all the more if they encounter Christians and proclaimers of the Gospel who place a high value on all forms of service, and link them with talk about God in the context of the Jewish-Christian tradition; though this link may be either explicit, or forged through the recognition and gift of loving service.

7. THE USE OF THEOLOGY

But what use are these reflections of a 'practical theologian' in the context of the scholarly disciplines, with the diversified organisation prevailing there today? T. Zerfaß does not take a very exalted view of their usefulness, because in his view scholarly theology is too bookish and not contextual enough. Moreover he thinks that it is illusory for this theology to imagine that it can deepen the spiritual motivation of those concerned with it.[23] My own experience does not permit me any emphatic contradiction. And yet I am inclined not to set so little store by the reflections of university theology about service for others. After all, here a long overdue process is at last taking place within theology itself; for it is trying in its discussions to arrive at a high argumentative, theological assessment of *diakonia*. And up to now we have found nothing of the kind in even one per cent of theological literature.[24]

Apart from this clarification of the significance of service in theology's own field, I should not like either to discredit the—at least possible—effect of these endeavours, an effect which is also continually experienced in the relevant encounters. For one result is that the people engaged in pastoral care and proclamation are attaching increasing importance to this kind of ministry (or at least pay it lip service). And this means greater appreciation of all those in the congregation who perform the little and the greater services, and are involved in social work. A change, step by step, in the awareness and spirituality of theologians (men and women) and of clergy would perhaps be a fruitful beginning—provided that one believes that awareness has to some degree genuine power.

I believe too that it is not pure illusion to hope that theologians may enter into an exchange of views, for example with social workers, and that they may pass on their ideas as motivating help to the people concerned. But this exchange must be on equal terms and in the appropriate language. And it will be the more fruitful the more theologians allow themselves to be affected by what they are told about the social field involved. Perhaps we are after all gradually rediscovering common social sectors, where theological concepts make their impact, not as indoctrination and discipline, but as ideas, which put themselves at risk in confrontation with the narratives of those engaged in charitable service, and let themselves be forged by these people's experiences and opportunities for faith.

Ultimately speaking, 'contextuality' cannot be entirely denied to the theologians concerned with *diakonia*, because they themselves are often forced, with some anguish, to think anew about it, because of real experiences of personal suffering, and through the suffering of others. The reproach is of course still justified where this contextuality remains largely private, and does not enter explicitly into the publications of these theologians. That is no doubt connected with the nature of European theology, which is largely argumentative and not sufficiently 'narratively' sustained. This is probably the justifiable criticism of an insufficiently contextual theology: that individual contexts are insufficiently brought into the discussion of principles, and are insufficiently accepted. That is to say, they are not sufficiently used as starting point and tend to be forgotten in subsequent reflection. Yet these individual contexts have a dignity as 'arguments' of a special kind, for which rational argument is no substitute. One would often like to know even from theologian the places and starting point of their specific love.

This would in itself be the beginning of a change in theology from professionally academic thinking to personal and positional reflections in the context of individual experiences, not merely with books but also with human life and suffering. It would mean entering the context of some suffering people at least, and of corresponding projects near by, as well as entering into active and political solidarity with people far away. But certainly to achieve this, and with this in mind, European theologians would courageously have to try out and discover a new language. Even theologians belonging to the 'First World'—and they particularly—will need much conversion before they can press forward a theology which is there for other people, and which finds expression in ministry for others. But in entering on this path theology may perhaps become a driving force which—though its efficacy must not be overestimated—cannot be ignored in a Church that is there for others, and which is constituted through service for other people.

Translated by Margaret Kohl

Notes

1. See N. Brox 'Häresie' in *Reallexikon für Antike und CHristentum* (Stuttgart 1950–) VIII, 248–297; C. Colpe 'Die Ausbildung des Heidenbegriffs von Israel zur Apologetik und das Zweideutigwerden des Christentum' in R. Faber and R. Schlesier (ed.) *Die Restauration der Götter* (Würzburg 1986) pp. 61–87.

2. See P. Hoffmann 'Tradition und Situation' in K. Kertelge (ed.), *Ethik im Neuen Testament* (Freiburg 1984) pp. 50–118; M. Puzicha 'Zur Aufnahme der Fremden in der alten Kirche' in O. Fuchs (ed.) *Die Fremden* (Düsseldorf 1988) pp. 180–183.

3. See Brox 'Häresie' *op. cit.* 255ff.; J. Becker 'Feindesliebe—Nächstenliebe—Bruderliebe' *Evangelische Ethik* 25 (1981) pp. 1, 5–18, esp. 10ff., 16ff.

4. See Colpe, 'Heidenbegriff', *op cit.* pp. 72–82.

5. Cf. K. Lehmann 'Nochmals: Caritas und Pastoral' *Caritas* 88 (1987) pp. 1, 3–12, where it is not really clear where the main reference of the brotherly and ministering congregation lies. The general trend of the argument would suggest that it is *koinonia* rather than *diakonia*. This is shown, for example, by the use of the term 'all' in the following quotation: 'All are there for one another. All are members of the one body' (p. 9). On the mutual delimination between *koinonia* and *diakonia*, and their critical complementation, cf., also R. Zerfaß 'Der Beitrag des Caritasverbandes zur Ziakonie der Gemeinde' *Caritas* 88 (1987) pp. 1, 12–27, 19ff., 22ff.

6. The institutions of the freely sponsored welfare organisations (the sponsor in this case being the church) are 80 per cent financed by the state, the rest having to be supplied by the church from its own income (which results from church tax and voluntary contributions). Persons employed in the parishes and in special sectors of pastoral care amount to only about 10 per cent of the number employed in the Caritas organisation! But the corresponding awareness among those employed full-time in pastoral care and in theology is certainly in inverse proportion to this representation of the Church's ministry in society; for among theologians and those concerned in pastoral care, the Church's expression of itself through service is seldom discussed. On the history and development of the Caritasverband, and on its relationship to the congregations, cf., R. Zerfaß 'Organisierte Caritas als Herausforderung an eine nachkonziliare Theologie' in E. Schulz, H. Brosseder and H. Wahl (ed.) *Den Menschen nachgehen. Offene Seelsorge als Diakonie in der Gesellschaft* (St Ottilien 1978) 321–348.

7. See Lehmann 'Caritas', *op. cit.* pp. 6ff.

8. See Zerfaß 'Herausforderung' *op. cit.* pp. 336ff., 347ff.; O. Fuchs 'Der Wert des Lebens oder wie wertvoll ist das Leben?' *Caritas* 86 (1985) 2, pp. 65–78.

9. See Zerfaß 'Herausforderung' *op. cit.* 336ff., 341; O. Fuchs 'Kirchliche Gemeinde und Caritas im Selbstvollzug der diakonie: Christliches Leben mit HIV-infizierten und aidskranken Menschen' *Caritas* 88 (1987) 6, pp. 280–293.

10. See Zerfaß 'Herausforderung' *op. cit.* p. 334; also his 'Beitrag' *op. cit.* p. 14.

11. See U. Bach *Boden unter den Füßen hat keiner* (Göttingen 1980) pp. 70–83; Zerfaß 'Herausforderung' *op. cit.* pp. 346ff.

12. German text in *Verlautbarungen des Apostolischen Stuhls* No 72 (Bonn 1986).

13. Lehmann 'Caritas', *op. cit.* 11.

14. Ibid.

15. See O. Fuchs 'Jugend und Liturgie im Horizont der Evangelisierung' *Liturgisches Jahrbuch* 37 (1987) 3, 156, 187, 182ff.

16. I do not speak here of the invitation to *all* the suffering, or to all people of good will, to partake of the Eucharist, since this could also be interpreted as an appropriation of 'non-Christian' helpers or people in need. The Eucharistic celebration is a special sphere for the *koinonia* of the Church, where *all Christians* can assure themselves of God's unconditional grace and love for human beings, and where, in the power of this divine Spirit, they may be encouraged to practise similar

unconditional ministry towards others. But, as in the case of baptism and faith, this (restricted) sphere of participation in the sacramental life of the Church, with the resources conferred there, has as its purpose the passing on of what has been received—not through the strategy of 'compelling them to come in' but in outgoing love (cf. Zerfaß 'Herausforderung' *op. cit.* p. 344).

17. See Zerfaß 'Herausforderung' *op. cit.* p. 343: 'It is therefore theologically and pastorally atrocious to give the impression that it is not love that is the fulfilment of the law and the first of the commandments, but rather complete identification with the Church's doctrine of faith and morals.'

18. See Lehmann 'Caritas' p. 10.

19. On the relationship between evangelisation and service in the context of a possible European liberation theology, see O. Fuchs, '"Umstürzlerische" Bemerkungen zur Option der Diakonie herzulande' *Caritas '85*, Yearbook ed. by the Deutscher Caritasverband (Freiburg 1984) pp. 9–40. R. Zerfaß makes a similar plea for a European 'post-conciliar theology' which will view itself and realise itself contextually against the background of service for others. See Zerfaß 'Herausforderung' *op. cit.* pp. 324, 338ff.

20. Contrary to Lemann 'Caritas', p. 11, and also to P. Zulehner *Das Gottesgerücht* (Düsseldorf 1987) p. 65.

21. See Zerfaß 'Beitrag' p. 20; also his 'Herausforderung' pp. 342–348 esp. 343 and 344.

22. On this 'material hermeneutics' cf., O. Fuchs 'Die praktische Theologie im Paradigma biblisch-kritischer Handlungswissenschaft zur Praxis der Befreiung' in O. Fuchs (ed.) *Theologie und Handeln* (Düseldorf 1984) pp. 209–244.

23. See Zerfaß 'Herausforderung' *op. cit.* pp. 324, 328–339.

24. Ibid. p. 323.

Frei Betto

The Prophetic Diakonia: The Church's Contribution to forming Humanity's Future

THE PROPHETIC diakonia of the churches is characterised by the service required by God through the signs of the times. This is something God imposes on us, irrespective of our merits, like the calling of the prophets. In the Third World this duty is called justice. The formation of the men and women of the future must inevitably include the phase of a social project in which the right to liberty is experienced as a requirement of justice. The Churches are no longer trying to look like catapults firing oppressors and oppressed up to heaven—with the obvious exception of the 'electronic' churches and sects, which are an instrument of US policy (set out in the Santa Fe Document which defines foreign policy for the Reagan administration in this area) designed to stem the advance of Christian base communities and liberation theology, particularly in Latin America.

The kingdom of God is already present amongst us who find ourselves in this place where grace is at work articulating the saving project: history. The future that lies 'over the hills' is reached by way of the future that lies 'just ahead of us'. This Christian understanding of history grows from the same Judaic roots that later influenced Marxism. Yahweh, as opposed to other gods, does not create through one final and instantaneous act: the predominant note in the Genesis account of creation is its temporality—the seven days. So, even before evolution reached its peak in the appearance of a consciousness that not only knows, but also—and above all—knows that it knows, there was already an historical dynamism in nature as the process through which God is made present and sows the first-fruits of God's promise.

For the churches to live the prophetic diakonia in the Third World today they must once again adopt the kerygmatic practice of John the Baptist: conversion must be translated into a struggle for justice (Luke 3:7–18). The difficulty for them lies in the linkage between faith and politics. For Catholics, for example, the social teaching of the Church tends toward the establishment of islands of justice within the capitalist system which, as its name indicates, implies the priority of capital (and profit) over labour (and workers). In many countries this Utopian vision has been deeply conditioned by the historical, social and ideological conditions into which the Church has been inserted. These are nations in which the Church has taken on the role of mediator between the bourgeois State and the people, or of religious legitimiser of the ruling structures, tasks for which it has been paid in the form of tax exemptions, special status with regard to its property or even the inclusion of its clergy on the public payroll.

Such factors limit the prophetic freedom of the Church and its powers of discernment in the face of the challenges posed by the future. A church that thinks on the basis of a social situation regarded as universal and abstract, is in fact a church thinking on the basis of its own institutional interests. But the prophetic office is always an exclusive reference to God starting from the rights of the poor. Those churches that find themselves tied to the project of the bourgeois state develop a thick ideological overlay that tends to cover the profession of faith. An example of this would be their support of anti-communism in the name of a basic option for human rights: what rights and what humans? These are usually the rights found in bourgeois societies: elections, freedom of the press, opposition parties, and the like. These are worthy objects, but the exercise of such freedoms has not led to greater social justice in the capitalist countries or to real sharing by the people in the exercise of State power. On the contrary, formal democracy has served to disguise the complete hegemony exercised by the capital-owning class over the rest of society. The supposedly freest nation—the United States—is undoubtedly the one that most oppresses the Third World.

In this part of the world, the struggle is for basic rights: to life, to food, to health, to education, to work and the rest. It is a fact that only in Socialist countries is the basic right to life assured for the vast majority of the population without the resources for this coming from profit derived from the exploitation of the Third World. To say that these basic rights are also assured for the vast majority of the populations of the Western European or Scandinavian countries is undoubtedly true, but raises the further question: is this derived from the work done by their own populations or from the exploitation of other countries by their businesses and banks? In 1986 alone,

Latin America had an outflow of 153 billion dollars from transfer of royalties, profits and capital. In 1988 the Third World will have to transfer 145 billion dollars into the coffers of banks in the developed world, in the form of interest payments on its external debt.

1. PEACE AS THE FRUIT OF JUSTICE

Forming new men and women is a service that includes the pursuit of peace. This will always be fragile while it remains a mere balance of power. It should be the fruit of justice, as Paul VI said. Even if Reagan and Gorbachev were to sign a treaty eliminating all the nuclear arsenals that threaten humanity with extinction, this would be important but not enough. On the periphery of the world, the nuclear bomb has already exploded in the shape of what destroys our economies and stifles our populations with ever-growing poverty: the external debt. Here, the name of peace is written with the word 'bread'. In this respect, the Christian symbol of the Cross expresses the peace programme: co-existence between the two arms, East and West, based on the destruction of nuclear weapons, needs to be complemented with new criteria of justice for dealings between North and South, based on a new international economic order. Otherwise, peace will be no more than a piece of paper signed by the superpowers. Today, the technological advances in the field of the mass media have reduced the world to a global village. The TV screen brings what is happening to our neighbour, be he or she in Nicaragua, South Africa or Afghanistan, straight into our homes. Any regional conflict immediately and inevitably has international repercussions and implications.

Breaking down barriers that stand in the way of peace—including social inequalities in the Third World—and building a just system is a task intrinsic to the evangelical mission of the churches. Such a challenge can only be translated into effective historical action through their pastoral strategies. Salvation is not something that belongs exclusively to the next life. It is substantially communion between persons and God and communion of persons among themselves, persons situated and permeated by social, economic and political structures. Therefore, salvation is something that is decided here and now (Mark 1:15), in the measure that human reality is transformed and taken up into its fulness in Christ (Rom. 8:20–21). In this sense, sin—which is always a form of alienation—is not just something that prevents communion between humanity and God. It is also whatever hinders communion of persons among themselves (Mark 10:17–21). Therefore, salvation is a challenge set within history, politically articulated, and which the Bible calls liberation (Exod. 3:7–10; Luke 4:18–19).

In the Third World, the conquest of justice supposes an integral liberation. This is not an academic or abstract question. Here, oppression impregnates institutions, laws, structures and governments, and shows itself in collective deprivation, in high indices of infant mortality, in the genocide of indigenous tribes, in discrimination against blacks, in subordination of women and exploitation of workers. The most shameful realisation is that such mechanisms of domination and death are held in place by classes and public authorities that, especially in Latin America, call themselves Christian. ...

2. THE OPTION FOR THE POOR

If they are to be clear with regard to the priorities for their diakonia in the social and historical process, the churches need to subject themselves to a deep and critical process of theological and theological discernment. To know God is to practise justice (Jer. 22:16). The injustice that predominates in the Third World is an objective negation of the God of life revealed in Jesus. In this context, it is not philosophical atheism that is the enemy of the Gospel, but idolatry with its worship of the false gods raised up by the consumerism of capitalist society: gods that can only be kept alive by the permanent sacrifice of the lives of the poor.

In the light of Christian faith, the poor are a prophetic reality in themselves. Both the Old and New Testaments show that the achievement of God's justice in history is rooted in the liberation of the poor. The poor are the sacrament of Christ in history (Matt. 25:31–46). The very God, in Jesus, became poor (Phil. 2:6–11) and proclaimed liberation from all forms of domination—the fruits of sin—as the definitive criterion for the manifestation of the Kingdom (Luke 3:7–14; 4:18–19). The Father's preference for these sons and daughters is not based on their being better or worse than other people; it is based simply on the fact of their being poor, that is, having been impoverished as victims of injustice. The Puebla Conference identified the face of Christ in the faces of the poor of Latin America (33). So, liberating the oppressed is the sign of the newness of the Gospel message (Luke 1:46–55), the basic requirement of the beatitudes (Matt. 5:1–12; Luke 6:20–23) and the first condition for following Jesus (Mark 10:17–22). In the Gospel there is no possibility of becoming a follower or disciple of Jesus without first practising justice and sharing goods (Luke 3:7–14).

For the Churches, their option for the poor, as a sign of their prophetic diakonia, should be seen as an imperative to break with the dominant forces and classes responsible for the death of the poor. It should furthermore induce them to commit themselves to those social forces that have come to the fore in the struggles for liberation in the Third World. Those who are not engaged in the building of this project of justice and peace that the Gospel calls the kingdom of God should not consider themselves disciples of Jesus. In our present context, 'kingdom' does not have the semantic force it did when emplyed in the context of first-century Palestine. There, proclaiming a kingdom that was not that of Caesar amounted to the same as is implied today in Latin America in defending a different political regime from that which corresponds to the interests of North American imperialism.

This means that Jesus' liberating purpose, summed up in the 'Utopian' category of the kingdom, admits no abstractions. It coincides with the justice that makes the poor recover life (John 5:8; 10:10). Such a practice is a political threat to the ruling order and is what determined Jesus' condemnation to death (John 11:49–50). In Latin America today, Jesus' sacrifice is prolonged in the martyrdom of all those who devote their lives to seeking first the kingdom of God and its justice: Archbishop Romero, Camilo Torres, Gaspar García Laviana, Frei Toto and so many other anonymous combatants. This includes all those who do not profess the Christian faith explicitly, but who are nevertheless united to Christ through their disinterested and loving service in the cause of the struggle that seeks to eradicate capitalist domination and create a new social order based on the spirit of brother-and sisterhood (1 Cor. 13:2; 1 John 4:7–21).

3. FORMING NEW MEN AND WOMEN

While on one hand the conquest of liberation and peace in the Third World requires the Christian churches to make a definite commitment to replacing the capitalist system of domination and forming a fraternal society, on the other, we should not fall into the illusion—even while recognising the undeniable social advances brought by Socialism—that implanting socialist regimes will mean the success of the liberation project. If it is to be authentic and complete, liberation has to move from the sphere of necessity to that of freedom, has to embrace everything from the inner nature of individuals to their most social dimension, has to link economics with spirituality, has to be built on solid and unquestionable ethical and moral foundations.

The Hymn to Love in 1 Corinthians 13:1–13 is undoubtedly the best portrait ever drawn of the new men and women, liberated from the sphere of egoism and immersed in the dynamic of love. It is often said of the Christian base communities of Latin America that they spring from a marriage between St Teresa of Avila and Ernesto 'Che' Guevara. ... The image seeks to portray the objective and subjective dimensions of the same liberating process. For

Paul, in Corinthians, these future human beings will not be presumptuous, nor use their wisdom and scientific learning for purposes not dictated by criteria of love; the socialisation of goods will not be a mere political-administrative project. The new men and women will be patient and generous, their hearts purified of traces of envy, ostentation and power-seeking; they will do nothing to harm others and will not seek their own interests; they will not be hot-tempered or bear a grudge; they will never rejoice at injustice, but their joy will be in proclaiming truth; their whole beings will overflow with love.

The processes of economic and political reform recently set in motion in some Socialist countries is nothing more than a recognition that till now their regimes have not succeeded in facing up to their main challenge: the human factor. It is not enough to create socialising structures: what has to be done is to form people who, in their relationships and activities, are capable of putting *us* first instead of *me*. Fidel Castro, addressing the fifty-third Plenary of Cuban Workers on 14 January 1987, warned that 'the socialist formula can lead to egoism and individualism if people are told every day only what they can earn from what they do'. The commemoration of the thirtieth anniversary of the 'Granma' landing, in December 1986, produced a new aphorism in Cuba: 'Now we are really going to build socialism'. At the time I was in the diocese of Camaguey, at the invitation of Bishop Adolfo Rodríguez, President of the Bishops' Conference, and on my return to Havana, I decided to carry out a little enquiry. I asked my communist friends: 'When will you be able to say "Now we have really built socialism"?' Some replied: 'When we have overcome all material needs'. So is socialism, finally, the dream of every citizen living like a bourgeois? 'Suppose', I said to them, 'that Cuba reaches a level of development that permits all its citizens full access to superfluous consumer goods. Will this be the realisation of the socialist ideal? Then suppose that at some point in the future there is a massive attack or an ecological catastrophe that so affects the productive system that the population's standard of living is set back thirty years. Will socialism also move back thirty years?'

For both Christianity and Marxism, what determines the quality of the future is the advent of new men and women. In the same address, Castro recognised that 'socialism is far from being a totally just and perfect society. I cannot see how to achieve this except through development of conscience, of high moral concepts, high human concepts, high concepts of solidarity and political ideals, going beyond maximum development of productive forces'.

In his closing speech to the Third Cuban Communist Party Congress on 2 December 1986, the Cuban leader criticised 'the blind belief ... that the building of socialism is, basically or essentially, a question of mechanisms. ... I believe that the building of socialism and communism is, essentially, a political and a revolutionary task, that is has basically to be the result of developing people's consciousness and educating them for socialism and communism. ... The political task is not to read people, day after day, a catechism on Marx and Lenin, but to be capable of awakening their human and moral motivations.'

In his address to the Plenary Session of the Central Committee of the Communist Party of the USSR, on 27 January 1987, Mikhail Gorbachev expressed the same point of view when he said that, seventy years after the October Revolution, socialism could make no further progress in the USSR if questions of political education and ethical priorities were not faced with boldness and frankness. 'Renewal', he said 'involves freeing society completely from the equivocations of socialist morality and firmly applying the principles of social justice; ensuring unity between what is said and what is done, between rights and duties; rewarding high quality honest work and doing away with salary-levelling and consumerist tendencies. I believe the objective of transformation is obvious: basic renewal of all aspects of the country's life, endowing socialism with the most modern forms of social organisation and fully displaying the humanitarian nature of our system in its decisive aspects: economic, social, political and ethical.'

When leaders as important as Fidel Castro and Mikhail Gorbachev encourage their people to a basic self-criticism, to a process of rectification and renewal that breaks with mechanistic formulas and overthrows dogmatic positions, concentrating their attention on the challenge of forming new men and women, theology cannot but identify this ethical purpose as a privileged framework of convergence for the achievement of God's plan in history. We stand at the gate of a new century and the threshold of a new age, when liberation will be more than a political project of social change, when it will become a spiritual project too, a loving basis for human relationships, for sharing the fruits of nature and the products of human work, for selfless dedication and international solidarity, for the possibility of human beings transcending themselves so as to discover, at the heart of their personal and historical existence, the ineffable presence of God.

In this process, we Christians have the evangelical duty to witness to the God of life in effective commitment to all those who struggle for the liberation of the oppressed. In this prophetic diakonia, our churches must move beyond triumphalisms and rivalries, hegemonic temptations and presumptuous monologues, abandoning all debate over who is for Paul and who for Apollo (cf., 1 Cor 3:3–4). In the spirit of Christ, they must rediscover their unity in an ecumenical attitude, superseding doctrinal debates, based on the practice of charity through militant solidarity in the cause of a future in which difference no longer means divergence. We should not forget that God also works through the love and works of those who, for the present, know God only in the poor to whom they give bread and the oppressed whom they liberate (Matt. 25:31–46). If we want to renew the face of the earth, win justice and enjoy peace, we must first ask what we can do for the best, whom we should serve first, where we can be most useful, not to the interests of our churches, but to the aspirations and hopes of our peoples.

Translated by Paul Burns

PART III

Areas of Conflict in Diaconal Praxis

Hermann Steinkamp

Diakonia in the Church of the Rich and the Church of the Poor: A comparative Study in Empirical Ecclesiology

A COMPARISON between the diakonia of the 'Churches of the rich', for example that of West Germany, and the caring work of the 'Churches of the poor',[1] for example that of Brazil, is at the moment not just of (relatively timeless) academic theological interest: it is in fact imposing itself on us in view of an acute sharpening of the dilemmas of what has been termed the structural parallelism[2] of the two large national Churches in West Germany. A recent empirical investigation of the situation of the Evangelical Church and in particular its membership[3] has revealed the following set of circumstances. The Church is perceived by the majority of 'normal', 'healthy' working people aged between 20 and 50 as something which 'is there above all for those who 'need' it somehow or other as a help and support. It ought to be there for those who can no longer or cannot yet correspond to the ideal of the working adult'.[4] It is precisely for these reasons that this group feels distance and alienation with regard to the Church: it feels it is not being addressed by it.,

What does this mean? Let us begin by simplifying. The centuries old structural division into an 'inside' organised in parish communities and emphasising preaching and worship and a (caring) 'outside'—a division reinforced since the middle of the nineteenth century[5]—has finally led to many nominal members of the national church knowing only the 'outside' of the Church, its most plausible aspect in the eyes of secular society, and accepting it as such, but no longer experiencing it as affecting themselves, i.e., as members of a parish.

We are becoming aware of these effects of a structural vicious circle at a time when in the churches of the Third World, including Brazil, Christian base communities are developing an attraction no longer experienced since the early Church. Even for Europe they are turning into a kind of symbol of hope, and from them many Christians long for a re-awakening of the national church.

The aim of what follows is to expound the connection I have roughly outlined above. The comparison starts from the hypothesis that the 'rich Churches' can perceive themselves in a more theologically suitable way in the mirror of the 'poor Churches'.[6]

1. THE AMBIVALENCE AND DILEMMAS THAT ARISE WITH INSTITUTIONALISED DIAKONIA

(a) The history of the problem

The structural splitting off of the dimension of caring activity from that of worship or preaching—things which still formed an unbroken unity in what Jesus did—is something that begins right at the start of the Church, first of all with the differentiation of the roles of the 'twelve' and of the 'college of seven' (Acts 6:1–6), later with that of the roles of the episkopos, presbyter and diakonos. If the 'ministry of the Word' and the 'ministry of tables' were at first merely two functions within the same meal-assembly, the splitting off the *agape* from the Lord's supper marked the formation of the germ of that structural parallelism which has continued to have its effects until our own day.[7]

The most radical sociological intensification of the separation of worship and diakonia came about with the Constantinian shift to the imperial Church with neglect of the *koinonia* that characterised the Church of the minority: 'The sumptuousness of the court ceremonial with which the clergy surrounded its liturgical activity made its contribution towards alienating from each other worship and the social dimension of the old community assembly ... : the loss of *koinonia* on the part of the caring dimension the social disintegration of worship.'[8] The Church's organised diakonia was shortly to take over the State's duties of caring for the poor. Until the late middle ages this did not become a theological problem because the ideology of throne and altar naturally also regarded diakonia as unquestionably 'Christian' (in motivation).

Nevertheless, alongside this very early tendency towards the 'secularisation' in practice of the function of diakonia a second structural line can be traced back to the period before Constantine. Whether it was to supplement the lack or insufficiency of activity on the part of the State or the state Church, or whether it was a form of criticism motivated by the Gospel of the latter's tendencies towards secularisation, this continually sought to organise authentic caring. This line leads from the early diaconal institutions in Rome, hospitals and religious orders (the mendicant orders and the orders of knights) via the brotherhoods of the later middle ages and the post-Tridentine renaissance of the function of caring to the orders found by St Vincent de Paul and other charismatic personalities (Sisters of Charity, Sisters of Mercy). This tradition of the continual re-emergence of organised diakonia, the impulse springing up in a series of new forms to encounter Christ in the poor, can be read as a history of the 'Church of the poor' within the 'Church of the rich' (imperial Church, State Church).

The present pattern of the 'parallel structure' of diakonia in the two major West German Churches and their welfare organisations is likewise due to initiatives by lay-people and by pastors committed to the diaconal ministry of service (Wichern and others) around the middle or end of the nineteenth century: the founding in 1849 of the *Innere Mission* of the Evangelical Church and of the Catholic *Caritas-Verband* in 1987.

Implicit especially in the foundation of the *Innere Mission* was criticism of the bureaucractic ossification of the Prussian state Church, which—just like the Catholic Church for the different reason of its being embroiled in the *Kulturkampf*—was not able to meet the challenges of the workers' movement. This can be attributed to the 'counter-movements' with their emphasis on good works: over the centuries in a western Church which was conceived as 'official' and stood completely on the side of the ruling classes these continued Jesus's style of caring for people—admittedly as a 'parallel structure', and this too admittedly in the sense of a secondary or supplementary function.

(b) Present problems

Since the end of the second world war the institutionalised diakonia of the churches has been given a tremendous boost by the fact that it has become the official partner of the State's welfare work. The Catholic *Caritasverband* and the *Diakonisches Werk* of the Evangelical Church represent, alongside other welfare associations, fundamental structural elements, on the basis of the principle of subsidiarity, of the welfare state.

In this function the major churches in West Germany are not only visibly present in public awareness but in this they continue to share in the power and controlling function of the State.[9] This power of the churches may be less visible in contrast to earlier periods of co-operation between Church and

State, but through their welfare associations it has its effects on social policies and politics.[10] Not least because of their large welfare institutions (hospitals, old people's homes, children's homes, etc.) the churches are among the most important employers (while the relationship between 'Church' and 'welfare' workers amounts roughly to one third to two thirds). With the continual expansion of institutionalised diakonia (which is judged with general approval by secular society) goes an equally continuous decline in taking part in Church life in the parish. The two structures in which the Church is present in society are developing away from each other. This is shown particularly by the long-term change in motivation of Church members. In this connection J. Degen[11] draws the following three conclusions from the latest survey by the Evangelical Church in Germany (1984) into Church membership:

(i) 'this perspective (see above) the Church is a diaconal service enterprise for its own members.'

(ii) 'The Church is (or should be) not only a diaconal service enterprise for its own members: it is this too within society and by intention for all citizens whether or not they belong to the Church.'

(iii) 'With regard to the social services it peforms the Church is to a considerable degree interchangeable with State ... institutions and the latter's current aims and methods.[12]

If at first sight these findings could be given a positive valuation, on the lines of the image of the 'Church for others' or the caring (diaconal) Church', when analysed more closely they reveal a series of dilemmas. In place of being affected and disturbed by the Gospel many Church members have developed a kind of Maecenas mentality with regard to the Church as a service enterprise: through membership and paying one's church tax one supports a charitable institution with which otherwise one hardly still identifies oneself. 'To exaggerate slightly, without the caring dimension even more of the 'undecided' (the category used by the Evangelical survey mentioned above, indicating something like a latent readiness to walk out of the Church) would leave the Church even more quickly; at the same time a certain perception of caring work (looking after old people, the disadvantaged, etc.) is a considerable obstacle to identification for people who prefer to regard themselves as independent and standing on their own feet.'[13]

The dilemma of the 'churches of the rich' and its diakonia does not consist of its not doing sufficient caring, not being active for the world. It consists of the fact that this caring work is not borne by the people of God, by the congregation, but by a staff, a bureaucratic organisation. When looked at more closely this diaconal apparatus arouses the suspicion of being a 'colossus on weak legs'.[14] The dilemma is the splitting off of the community: it seems as if in this way, despite all the historical continuity of the problem, it has reached an extreme in our days. The more diakonia becomes professionalised the bureaucratised the less it seems to be borne by the faith and love of the people of God. And the other way round: the more the awareness prevails in congregations that their caring function, which in principle is something they cannot renounce, is already being taken over by specialists, the more this mentality of delegation and surrogacy spreads among normal members of congregations, the more the life of the average parish is reduced to worship, preaching and pious associations.[15] Already ten year ago Jürgen Moltmann suggested as a way out of these dilemmas a 'diaconisation of the parish community' and a 'congregationalisation of the diakonia',[16] but clearly the socio-historical and socio-psychological factors at work develop the kind of individual dynamism that cannot be changed by theological and pastoral appeals.

The dilemma is further intensified by the fact that the leadership of the churches do not get any help from theology when it comes to mastering this complexity analytically and drawing the necessary consequences. It is well known that the subject to the Church's caring dimension has been criminally neglected up till now, while the scientific discipline that could be termed 'diaconics' exists as an outsider in theological faculties.[17]

In this context the following theological questions centred on the dilemmas surrounding the parallel structure are among those in urgent need of theological investigation:

Can or must the dichotomous structure that grew up at the latest following the Constantinian revolution of diaconal initiatives and social patterns on the one hand and prish ones on the other be understood as ecclesiogenesis in the sense that the Church finds itself still on the way towards the 'caring community'?

Why are the non-parochial social patterns of caring activity (religious orders, brotherhoods, associations, etc.) not understood as communities or congregations?[18] What role is played in this connection by the (contingent) development of the Western priesthood?

Does the dichtomy of diakonia and parochial structures represent the continuation of the tension between worship and prophecy that characterised Judaism? If this is so, what is the significance of the bureaucratic ossification of charitable work?

These questions are once again not academic and timeless but very topical. They arise particularly against the background of the way of life of the 'Church of the poor' of Brazil, its option for the poor, its base communities and its liberation theology.

2. THE OPTION FOR THE POOR AS DIAKONIA

The distinction between the diakonia of the rich Church (of West Germany) and the poor Church (of Brazil) that precedes and underlies all the detail consists of the latter's option for the poor. This option characterises and comprises the caring dimension of the poor Churches. The distinction between this and the caring dimension of the rich Churches is made clear particularly by three subtle aspects of the help provided or the motivation for doing so.

(a) Solidarity instead of support

The option for the poor made by the Church of Brazil[19] has its effects not only in pastoral but also and primarily in political activity. It means a change of class position with far-reaching consequences for the relationship between Church and society. By renouncing social privileges, by renouncing sharing in the power of the State, the Church can the more credibly commit its moral and prophetic authority to the struggle for justice.

The difference in terms of empirical ecclesiology between this and the situation of the Church of the rich (c.f., West Germany) is clearly highlighted at the moment by the latter's half-heartedness or inability to put itself at the side of the 'new poor', the unemployed, immigrants, etc., who are suffering from the consequnces of mass unemployment. The Caritas-Verband and the Diakonisches Werk find that, precisely through their involvement in the organs of the welfare state, their hands are tied. They are structurally yoked into the bureaucratic apparatus for overcoming poverty and they cannot at the same time be the advocates of the poor, something that would be all the more necessary when the trade unions were not peforming this function.[20] To this extent the relationship of the rich Churches to the poor continues to remain marked by that fundamental attitude of concerned paternalism as has characterised the history of the western Church in general. What by contrast is meant by solidarity with the poor as it determined Jesus's life is something we can learn from the Churches of the Third World.

(b) Self-help v. professionalism

This applies too—and especially—to the actual pastoral practice of the poor Churches. The subjects of the annual *Camanha da Fraternidade* of the Brazilian bishops' conference place each time topical social needs at the centre of the Church's pastoral work, for example hunger in 1985, land reform in 1986, homeless children in 1987; and through this emphasis and concentration of forces these are given an unequivocally social and caring stress. In contrast internal Church matters like the administration of the sacraments, catechesis, etc., may not be relegated to the background but are orientated towards a political and diaconal emphasis. A typical example is the *romaria de terra*, a pilgrimage which links the traditional elements of pilgrimage with a kind of mass demonstration against the unjust distribution of the land. This kind of behaviour by the poor Church with its emphasis on practical caring 'avoids the misunderstanding that in its message it was ultimately only a question of words, thoughts, ideas, feelings, and at the most certain moral demands'.[21]

The pattern of behaviour that characterises all the Church's praxis in this field of pastoral caring is: supporting the struggle of those affected without taking it over and running it for them, enabling them to form a community and act in solidarity, and establishing the biblical message and tradition that God fights on the side of the dispossessed and oppressed.[22] These maxims for pastoral action go along with watchfulness against the danger of providing assistance for those affected in such a way as to render them incapable of running their own affairs, a danger that continually lurks within the professionalised welfare agencies in this country.[23] In contrast to this kind of diaconal praxis the compulsive attempt to distinguish between charitable and pastoral work reveals the local church as one whose concern for the continuance of its membership figures is greater than its concern for the justice of the kingdom of God.

Of course institutionalised welfare exists in Brazil in the form of the national Caritas organisation, a member of Caritas Internationalis. Its function and its relationship to the liberating, caring work of the Brazilian Church was described some years ago by Dom Fragoso, the Bishop of Crateús well known as the bishop of the poor: 'The Crateús diocesan office of Caritas belonged to the national association of Caritas. It received the supplies that came from the USA and did its best to distribute them according to the criteria of education for social development. The supplies consisted of the surplus from the agricultural production of the United States. If they had been stored in their country of origin, prices would inevitably have fallen, and there would have been a crisis. To dump them in the sea or burn them would have an international scandal. Being intelligent, as they are in the USA, they decided to send them as a gift to the countries of the Third World ... As those on the receiving end we became used simply to hold out our hands like beggars. With more than four hundred years of dependence round our shoulders we were immersed in the temptation to forget that man grows when he gives and not when he receives something he is given.[24]

It would be difficult to find a more striking description of the outline of diakonia when it is split off from koinonia and has degenerated into a caricature of Christian love of one's neighbour—despite all the worthy subjective motives that sustain it. The conclusion drawn by the Bishop of Crateús and his fellow-workers in the pastoral field pointed the way for the Brazilian Church's praxis based on reflection on liberation theology. After a period of distributing the gifts 'we got together and drew up a balance sheet from the educational point of view of this welfare work, including the receiving ... of supplies. We came to the conclusion that we were giving more help to the USA than to ourselves. So we decided no longer to accept this aid ..., and we preferred to put an end to Caritas.'[25]

(c) Konionia as the original form of diakonia: the base communities

The most striking difference between the caring work of the rich and the poor Churches can be seen from the practice of the base communities. They embody the ideal of a caring Church: in the way in which they live their faith and their practical concern one can see the way in which a caring Church emerges (ecclesiogenesis). In their theological understanding of themselves and in the way they live the base communities overcome and transcend two fundamental splits: the split between religion and the everyday world of society (faith and action, serving God and serving the world, Sunday and everyday religion, etc.); and the split between those who help and those in need of help.

(d) Base communities as a way of overcoming the parallel structure of diakonia

The structural splitting off the caring function produced by the history of the rich and pwerful western Church—a fundamental dilemma of parish organisation that has not yet been overcome—has been reintegrated in the base community: the unit of preaching, worship and diakonia. If there is a common theme to contemporary theological discussion of the dilemmas of the Church of the rich and its diakonia then it is the lament over the dispossession and incapacitation of the parish community with regard to its responsibility for caring, or over the loss of the dimension of kiononia by the Church's caring work.[26] The 'diaconisation of the parish community' or 'congregationalisation of diakonia' continually conjured up as suitable proposals for reform, sound like an impotent attempt to square the circle. What clearly represents an insoluble dilemma for the rich Churches has become in the base communities of the poor Churches a new reality that provides hope for the universal Church: the uniting of serving God and serving the world, the union of preaching, worship and caring, of proclaiming the kingdom of God and healing, as in the life and work of Jesus.[27]

(e) The primacy of koinonia

The base communities not only provide the universal Church at the moment with a plethora of patterns of collective identity but also give it a disarming freedom to call all possible associations of Christians communities, base communities. In the mirror of this way of life the problems of European Churches and theologians, with their distinction of parish and community, communities and 'paracommunities',[28] the parish community and the (welfare) association, brotherhood and religious order etc., have a compulsive effect.

Admittedly the theological distinction goes deeper. The base communities have (re-)discovered the primacy of koinonia over the other functions of the Christian community and have transcended the additive view of preaching, worship and diakonia in the primacy of koinonia. That has far-reaching consequences for the quality of their caring work. The difference that emerges in the various aspects of welfare and social work between those in need of help and those providing help, between those who give and those who receive, between professionals and clients, etc., is admittedly not eliminated in koinonia but is transcended in the preceding solidarity of those concerned, in the brotherly and sisterly sharing of need, joy and hope.

Further, the base community links the aspect of self-help with that of social commitment, in other words links service to one's comrades in the faith with solidarity with the poor in general. In the awareness of many base communities their roots in Brazil's revolutionary popular movements are as marked as their belonging to the Church. In the poor Churches there is no contradiction because their agenda is determined not by competition for numbers of members but by the strunggle for justice along with 'all men and women of good will' (*Gaudium et spes*). The base communities' capacity for koinonia is to that extent their diakonia, both internally and externally, as sharing and solidarity. Because of this radicality of their witness to the faith, their sharing and their solidarity with the poor, it would not be so simple to line them up in the tradition of the religious orders and thus to eliminate the thorn in the flesh of our Churches of the rich and their delegated charity.[29] The base communities of the poor Churches represent *the* challenge to the parishes of the Churches of the rich that have become dead as far as diakonia is concerned.

Translated by Robert Nowell

Notes

1. The verbal contrast between churches of the rich and churches of the poor is deliberate in its ambiguity. It makes sense in all conceivable aspects with regard to the two actual national Churches which this essay is concerned with.

2. The term coined by R. K. W. Schmitt in 1976 means, to simplify, the fact that characteristic of the institutional constitution of the churches of West Germany and their work of caring is their structural parallelism, in other words the removal, splitting off, or delegation of the work of caring from the Christian community and its organisation along more or less autonomous lines as in the Caritas-Verband or Diakonisches Werk.

3. *J. Hanselmann and others (ed.) Was wird aus der Kirche? Ergebnisse der zweiten EKD-Umfrage über Kirchenmitgliedschaft* (Gütersloh, 1984).

4. Ibid p. 44.

5. I. Lukatis and U. Wesenick (ed.) *Diakonie—Aussenseite der Kirche* (Göttingen, 1980).

6. The comparison with two national Churches should help to avoid sweeping statements about *the* rich or poor churches. It is assumed that the West German Church and its diakonia provides the ideal type, rather than the model, for a rich church.

7. For what follows see P. Phillipi '*Diakonie I*' in *Theologrsche Real—Enzyklopädie* (1981) pp. 644–656; U. Lück '*Nächstenliebe—ein traditionelles Thema im Abendland*' in A. Bellenbaum, H. J. Becker, and M. T. Gerven (ed.), *Helfen und helfende Berufe als soziale Kontrolle* (Opladen, 1985) pp. 1–27; W. Leise Geschichte der Caritas 2 volumes (Freiburg, 1922).

8. P. Philippi op. cit. p. 628.

9. See A. Bellenbaum H. J. Becker, and M. T. Greven, op. cit. (note 7 above) and also C. Sachsse and F. Tennstedt (ed.) *Soziale Sicherheit und soziale Disziplinierung* (Frankfurt, 1976) and their *Geschichte der Armenfürsorge in Deutschland, vom Spätmittelalter bis zum W Ersten Weltkrieg* (Stuttgart/Cologne/Mainz, 1980)

10. See H. Eyferth 'Geschichte: von der Armenpflege zum Sozialstaat', in Handbuch Sozialarbeit/Sozialpädagogik (Neuwied, 1984) pp. 430–438, 435.

11. See J. Degen *Diakonie im Widerspruch. Zur Politik der Barmherzigkeit im Sozialstaat (Munich, 1985)*.

12. *Op. cit. pp. 235–6.*

13. *H. Seibert 'Perspektiven der Diakonie' in M. Schick, H. Seibert, and Y. Spiegel (ed.) Diakonie und Sozialstaat* (Gütersloh, 1986) pp. 409–427, 414.

14. H.-J. Holzhauer '*Diakonie—Koloss auf schwachen Beinen? Ein Vergleich diakonierelevanter Aussagen in Demoskopie und Statistik. Tendenzen—Schlussfolgerungen*' in *Diakonia* 8 (1980) pp. 176–189.

15. See H. Steinkamp Diakonie—Kennzeichen der Gemeinde. Entwurf einer praktisch-theologischen Theorie (Freiburg, 1985).

16. See J. Moltmann *Diakonie im Horizont des Reiches Gottes* (Neunkirchen, 1984) p. 36, and also the contribution by N. Mette in this issue.

17. See J. Alber 'Diakonik-Geschichte der Nichteinführung einer praktisch-

theologischen Disziplin', in *Pastoraltheologie* 72 (1983), pp. 164–177 and P. Philippi
'*Diakonik—Diagnose des Fehlens einer Disziplin*', ibid. pp. 177–186.

18. See H. Eisenberg 'Kommunitäten—eine wiederentdeckte Berufung' in
T. Schober and H. Thimme (ed.) *Gemeinde in diakonischer und missionarischer
Verantwortung* (Stuttgart, 1979) pp. 227–231.

19. The fact that this does not apply to the entire Church of Brazil but to the great
majority of it at the present moment should be emphasised in this context against those
voices that reject from the start any reflection on the local 'class links of the Church'
(Y. Spiegel) with reference to national, social and economic developments in that
country.

20. See J. Strasser '*Sozialstaat*', in Handbuch Sozialarbeit/Sozialpädagogik
(Neuwied, 1984) pp. 1083–1101.

21. Karl Barth *Kirchliche Dogmatik*, vol. IV part 3 (Zürich, 1959) p. 1022.

22. See H. Steinkamp '*Wenn sich das Vorzeichen ändert*' in *Diakonia Christi* 22
(1987) no 3, pp. 12–13; see also his '*Die Reconquista der sem-terra-Bewegung und die
Pastoral da terra in Brasilien*' in H. Steinkamp, M. Estor and others *Die Zeichen der
Zeit deuten. Lernorte einer nachkonziliaren Sozialethik* (Münster, 1988).

23. See the forecast in *Entwicklung der freien Wohlfahrtspflege bis zum Jahr 2000*
(Basle, 1984) p. 40.

24. D. A. Fragoso *Befreiung vor Ord* (Mettingen, 1985) p. 25.

25. Ibid.

26. See F. J. Steinmeyer '*Die Kirche und ihre Diakonie in der Gesellschaft*' in
T. Schober and H. Thimme (ed.) op. cit. (note 18 above), pp. 306–317; J. Moltmann
op. cit. (note 16 above); P. Philippi *Diaconica* (Neunkirchen, 1984); and the
contribution of O. Fuchs in this issue.

27. See H. Seibert '*Gedanken zur theologischen Begründung gegenwärtiger Diakonie
durch den Bezug auf die Diakonie Jesu—Ein Plädoyer für eine exegetisch orientrte
Theologie der Diakonie*' in T. Schober and H. Thimme (ed.) *Theologie—Prägung und
Deutung der kirchlichen Diakonie* (Stuttgart, 1982) pp. 237–253, and their *Diakonie—
Hilfehandeln Jesu und soziale Arbeit des Diakonischen Werkes* (Gütersloh, 1983).

28. See W. Huber *Kirche* (Stuttgart/Berlin, 1979) p. 106.

29. That means to dispute their community quality by appealing to what is possible
for a national Church. On this see U. Duchrow '*Was können wir von den
Basisgemeinden in Brasilien Lernen?*' in *Pastoraltheologie* 75 (1986) pp. 229–248.

Norbert Mette

Solidarity with the Lowliest: Parish Growth Through the Witness of Practical Service

FOR SOME time now, discusson on practical theology in German-speaking countries has revolved increasingly around the inescapable connection between the diakonia of the Church and the parishes, and upon how this responsibility can be discharged in practice in the life of the Church.[1] This new emphasis is due to a variety of developments both in society and also in the Church. In briefest outline, here are some of them: (a) In society, problem situations brought about by structural changes both in society and in the economic sphere are affecting an increasing number of individuals and groups or whole classes of the population (the 'new poverty'),[2] whilst efforts inspired by neo-liberalism are being made to effect a fundamental change in the concept of the welfare state;[3] (b) In the Church, critical shortages of finance, personnel and other resources have posed with increasing urgency the question whether the enthusiastic postwar expansion of the commitment of the relief and social agencies of the Church to work in society may by now not only have overstepped the limits of its own available capacity, but whether it is in any event theologically justified.

Against this background expectant eyes are turned upon the local church parishes to see whether, if they regain an enhanced sense of their ineluctable responsibility for the work of the Church in society, they might be able to make a contribution in two spheres: first, by providing the necessary backup in terms of support and credibility to the social and relief work of the Church in society, and secondly by helping to invigorate the life of local communities, thus counteracting at least to some extent the disintegration of the structures of solidarity within society.

However, the call for greater integration of diakonia and parish often meets with a hesitant or even negative response. Fears may arise that this would promote a disastrous 'churchification' of the social and relief work; or else it is contended that such ideas are the result of romanticising the vocation of the Church in society, not taking sufficient account of the complex realities involved and of how the churches can best perform their social and relief functions therein. Doubts are also expressed as to whether there is any prospect of such 'diaconal' parishes actually coming into being within the existing Church.

These doubts and fears are not wholly without foundation. They do point to the fact that it clearly would not suffice just to aim at a greater integration of diakonia and the parishes as they are at the present moment. If well meant efforts of this kind are not to be doomed from the start, serious thought must be given to the question why diakonia and local parishes have followed such divergent paths as in large measure they have up to the present.

P. Philippi, the most knowledgeable writer on the diakonia of the Church in German-speaking areas, has suggested that the endeavour to give diakonia its rightful place in parish life will call for a fundamental paradigm shift both in outlook and in structure, which he summarises as 'away from parochialism to parish growth'.[4] He says that this is because the neglect of diakonia at parish level is by no means fortuitous, but is connected with the pastoral concept prevailing there. This, he says, is aimed primarily at giving pastoral care to individual church members on the local parish rolls, and it is far removed from the true idea of a 'parish'. The latter would come into existence only in so far as diakonia came to be recognised and practised as an indispensable, fundamental moment of the activity of the Church.

In the spirit of that assertion we shall try in what follows to explore some of the ways in which the diakonia of the Church and the growth of parishes belong together.

1. THE MARGINALISATION OF DIAKONIA IN THE PASTORAL WORK OF THE PRIESTHOOD

It would no exaggeration to claim, at least in German-speaking countries, that the pastoral work of Catholic priests is to a large extent dominated by a basically 'sacramentalist' outlook—the conviction that since the achievement of salvation depends almost exclusively on receiving the sacraments, the central task of pastoral work is to bring men and women as comprehensively as possible into contact with these healing agencies of the Church. 'Practising, in the sense of attending worship and receiving the sacraments, then becomes the supreme rule of living'.[5]

The stubborn persistence of this 'sacramentalism' may perhaps be traceable to two causes. First, it was for centuries the centre-piece of the Church's pastoral teaching[6] and as such was transmitted to the 'people of the Church'. And secondly, it appears to be very responsive to the deeply internalised expectations characteristic of 'popular religion' (P. M. Zulehner), particularly the need for the assurance in life-threatening situations of a transcendentally guaranteed place of refuge, an assurance aided by the performance of rituals.[7] Furthermore, it can be readily harmonised with a demand for religion latent in the secularised consciousness.[8] The social institution which corresponds to this pastoral concept is the 'pastorate', i.e. one appointed 'from on high' for giving spiritual and sacramental care to church members living within a circumscribed area through officially ordained ministers. The liturgical and sacaramental aspects have undisputed priority in their pastoral praxis, all other activities being oriented towards those aspects and deriving from them any importance they may have. Without the priest, consecrated and therefore set apart from the laity, nothing of consequence can happen in the pastorate.[9]

Cardinal Lorscheider has trenchantly defined the attitudes engendered by a pastoral concept of this kind: 'The pastorate was conceived as a structure designed to maintain and protect the faith in the midst of a Catholic population with markedly national characteristics. It is impossible to give it a missionary thrust' (or a social one—N. M.). It is the Christians belonging to the incumbency themselves who make it impossible. They don't want to give up their pastor for the benefit of others. So they don't allow him to go after the ninety-nine lost sheep, and they don't assist him in the search. All they want is to know that they are assured of their place in the sheepfold. Having the exclusive services of the priest is far more important to them than evangelising the nations. They endeavour at all costs to make sure that the services of the priest are directly available to each and every parishioner.[10] The individualistic understanding of salvation inherent in this idea of pastoral care ('save thine own soul!') has a direct effect on the place accorded to the social and relief work of the Church. The parson's remit does indeed include (hem. c. 468 CIC–1917) the 'fatherly care' of the poor, afflicted and sick within his parish; he should also give heed to the orgainsation and promotion of *opera caritatis, fidei et pietatis* (c. 469) and encourage laypeople also to be concerned for works of charity. But beyond any doubt, diakonia is not part of the 'proprium' of the pastoral ministry, but is of secondary importance; it is something akin to a 'proving ground' for the faithful, in which they can 'make their calling and election sure' by performing practical works of charity. The 'recipients' of these charitable services are regarded as objects; as in society, so in the parish and the church they are marginalised and not looked upon as organically belonging.

2. THE MARGINALISATION OF THE PASTORATE IN SOCIETY AND THE INSTITUTIONALISATION OF THE DIAKONA AS A 'SECONDARY STRUCTURE'

The pastoral concept of the 'pastorate' briefly sketched above has to be seen as a consequence of a structural change within society which has done away with that identity of the 'community of citizens' and the 'parish of Christians' on which the model of the parish was based. Originally it was this very model that provided a basis for the action of the church in the daily life of the community. The church formed an integral part of the total life of the community and put its stamp upon it, and hence no special emphasis on the care of the sick and afflicted was needed.

However, as the formerly unified structure of community life gradually gave way to a differentiated, pluralistic one, many of the presuppositions on which the parochial model had rested became invalid. The pastoral setup tried to react to this situation in a number of different ways. In some cases attempts were made to continue to give comprehensive care to church members, which could no longer be done with the outmoded social institutions of the parish alone, by setting up programmes, mostly directed towards specific groups, under the aegis of the church. One area of activity so affected was diakonia, which became separated out into an increasingly independent 'second structure' within the ecclesiastical praxis.[11]

While this was happening, the parochial model was not only left in being; it was given priority in pastoral matters, with the result that all other activity connected with the church was oriented to it and thus labelled as 'foreground'. This is often justified by a reference to the 'locality principle' for church action; but it does not avail to conceal the fact that many incumbencies have become 'rootless'. And the emphasis on the spiritual and sacramental aspects of the pastorate has further strengthened this trend. It permits individuals to be spiritually 'ministered to' without regard to their concrete relationships in society.

By contrast, many of the 'special' services of the Church which are peripheral to or even outside the pastorates exhibit direct contacts with contemporary lifestyles in all their variety. This applies particularly to extensive areas of the church's diakonia which come into daily contact with the various material and spiritual needs of people, most of whom cannot be reached by ordinary pastoral work. These activities truly show the church working 'on the ground'. Nevertheless, as long as pastoral work continues to be thought of in terms of the traditional stereotype, it will remain impossible to pay due regard to the theological and ecclesiological significance of the processes of individual caring and solidarity that are in train in this area. Yet the fact remains that those taking part in them often receive a lasting experience of the meaning of community in following Jesus, even if they do not manage to express it in ordered and explicit form.

It is therefore also not surprising that those engaged in diakonia frequently find it difficult to become established in the current pastorates because, with their own experiences, they are unable to be their old selves again. In this way, an ecclesial rootlessness of diakonia threatens to correspond to the social rootlessness of the pastorate.

3. 'PARISHING' AS THE PRAXIS OF DIACONAL SOLIDARITY

This disastrous drifting apart can only be countered by the reminder that the unity of parish and diakonia has been regarded as one of the central characteristics of Christian praxis since its beginnings. So, for example, there was apparently no problem for Ignatius of Antioch in using *agape* and *ekklesia* as synonymous concepts: 'The *agape* of Smyrna and Ephesus greets you', he writes to the parish of Tralles (13,1). *Agape* is here intended to express the solidarity manifesting itself in mutual support, a solidarity which unites the parishes with one another and is at the same time the hallmark of each individual parish.[12] *Agape* of this kind, as other early Christian writings impressively testify, gives birth to 'a "koinonia", a communal life in which all partake of the same possessions'.[13] It can therefore be said that 'diakonisation' and 'parishing' are two sides of the same process and are mutually dependent: where selfless action among human beings bears witness to and imparts God's love, there the parish of Jesus Christ is born.

In other words, togetherness (*Gemeinde* or *koinonia*) becomes visible as and when the diaconal work of the church is accompanied by a change or even a reversal of the usual patterns of thinking and acting, and new forms of social contact arise; when, for instance:

— need and suffering are no longer suppressed or minimised, but are approached with an awareness of their true nature.

— personal involvement in these things is not played down but acknowledged, but their socially induced causes are also disclosed and openly denounced.

— the part of the despised is taken even at the cost of being despised.

— the appearance of self-sufficiency is unmasked and one's own need of assistance is admitted.

— the usual role fixations of *helper* and *person in need of help* are abandoned.

— every effort is made to discover, develop and utilise the gifts and capabilities of the 'little people' which are readily written off.

— the 'God complex' of wishing and being able to heal everything is renounced in order to free oneself for insight into the precariousness of one's own efforts.

— situations in which by human standards 'nothing more can be done' are not avoided, but are worked through together with the sufferer.

Thus the diakonia of the Church extends to more than charitable actions performed occasionally from some religious disposition. It signifies getting alongside one's fellow men and women in practical ways inspired by the promise of a humanity made one in Christ, which brings people together across differences and boundaries, encourages them to act responsibly towards others and enables them to share with them.[14] Action of this kind, however fragmentary its successes may be, is what converts the fundamental Christian confession 'I believe that God loves you' from words into deeds. It is nourished by the recollection of the love of God as revealed in the self-emptying of Christ Jesus, and by trust in the efficacy of that love; otherwise it would remain a longing incapable of fulfilment. Such acts witness to this love, not create it.[15] This praxis finds its quintessential expression in the celebration of the Lord's Supper, in which the table fellowship with all which he promised and inaugurated is remembered and anticipated. I Cor. 1:11 says that where this does not take place in the physical presence of the least and the rejected ones and in visible koinonia with them, it is not a true eucharistic celebration—a verdict that is very appropriate when applied to a cultic practice motivated by the desire for individual salvation and centred on the sacrament, such as is not infrequently encountered.

4. 'DIAKONISATION' OF THE PARISH—'PARISHING' OF THE DIAKONIA

Without diakonia, then, there is no fellowship in the footsteps of Jesus, but at best parishes only too ready to use a reference to the manifold charitable activities of the Church, and their financial support of such activites, as an alibi for their own 'pious self-sufficiency'. Conversely there is a risk that the diakonia of the Church may be losing its roots there, and that the agencies may increasingly tend to become just one more autonomous service undertaking aided by the welfare state.

This being so, what is needed is a dual process of learning and transformation which J. Moltmann has well characterised as ' "Diakonisation" of the parish' (a) and ' "Parishing" of the diakonia' (b):[17]

(a) The parochial model has the basic advantage that action by the church continues to be in touch with the communal interrelations within a given local community which obey a different set of presuppositions. However, as long as pastoral care has the individualistic reference of the traditional pattern it is difficult to foster awareness of the church's responsibility for this common life. Therefore 'diakonisation of the parish' involve making a decisive break with such a concept. Then attention is no longer directed to an individual reduced to an abstract inwardness; instead the physical need, spiritual stress and social injustice which can be encountered in the immediate surroundings in which individuals or groups are living, form the focus for thought and action.

Such a process is most likely to crystallise around those groups within the established parishes which are living a fringe existence—groups which have committed themselves to a regime of diakonia in solidarity and are endeavouring to put it into practice. If it is desired to make a fresh start in which the parish and the social agencies of the church are taken seriously in their mutual interrelatedness, and then to see the local community as a challenge to adequate practical commitment, then an indispensable first step is to cease marginalising such groups, and instead to give full scope to their indispensable role as constituents of the parish, even though this may often lead to conflicts on account of their at times 'uncomfortable' commitment.[18]

(b) But this mutual interrelatedness does not exist only at the level of the local church parish. Because of the many aspects of suffering and need in a society which has become transparent, the diakonia of the Church must be organised regionally and nationally and must have a differentiated structure, able to call upon the necessary professional skills, if it is to be able to carry out certain aid operations responsibly or call attention to wrong developments in the social structure. And yet in many instances it has turned into a 'social relief agency', paralleling the prevailing concept of the 'caring pastorate'. In contrast, ' "parishing" of the diakonia' is a recall to the 'unrenounceable self-demand in all social work for which the Church accepts responsibility—namely that the parish dimension is involved right from the start in any and every work of healing, comforting and assisting, and this for the sake of people needing help, for the sake of the helpers, and for the sake of a growing solidarity for those who receive help and those who give it'.[19] 'Parishing' does not mean organising additional activities within the diakonia of the church, labelled 'religious'. What it means is that all those involved shall be able to experience togetherness (koinonia) to the extent that they learn to see themselves as a 'fellowship of those accepted by Christ who accept one another' (cf. Rom. 15:7) 'in which the weak and the strong, healthy and sick, able and disabled, live together and serve each other with the gift they have received (cf. 1 Pet. 4:10)'.[20].

Translated by Alan Braley

Notes

1. See literature surveys on this subject by H. Theurich 'Gemeindediakoine', in *Handbuch der Praktischen Theologie* Vol. 3, (Gütersloh 1983) 497–511, here 509ff. and E. Steinkamp *Diakonie—Kennzeichen der Gemeinde* (Freiburg 1985) 117–123.

2. On this see article by G. Baum in this issue.

3. On this see article by J. Degen in this issue.

4. P. Philippi *Diaconie. Über die soziale Dimension kirchlicher Verantwortung* (Neukirchen-Vluyn 1984) 38; cf. also 20–20. 37–48.

5. J. Bommer 'Lernort Geimeinde: Gemeinde lernen im Glauben' in *KatBl* 108 (1983) 114–121, here: 116. Cf. also P. M. Zulehner *Denn Du kommst unserem Tun mit deiner Gnade zuvor ...* (Düsseldorf 1984) esp. 32ff.; E. Sauer 'Evangelisierung statt Sakramentalisierung?' in W. Eckermann et al (Hg.) *Sakramente—Heilzeichen für das Leben der Welt* (Cloppenburg 1987) 159–174, esp. 160–164.

6. The authoritative text for this is to be found in CIC–1917, esp. cc. 465–470.

7. See P. M. Zulehner loc. cit. 34f.

8. see J. B. Metz *Glaube in Geschichte und gesellschaft* (Mainz 1977) esp. 29ff. 57ff.

9. See also L. Boff *Kirche: Charisma und Macht* (Düsseldorf 1985) 18f.

10. A. Lorscheider *Die Pfarrie* in *Weltkirche* 5 (1985) 23f.

11. See E. Steinkamp, loc. cit. 43ff.

12. See cf. J. Comblin *Das Bild vom Menschen* (Düsseldorf 1987) 21f.

13. Loc. cit. 21.

14. See J. Wanke *Der Weg der Kirche* in B. Kresing (Pub.) *Für die Vielen* (Paderborn 1984) 256–270, esp. 266f.

15. See Th. Proepper *Erlösungsglaube und Freiheitsgeschichte* (Munich 1985) esp. 106ff.

16. See M. Barth *Das Mahl des Herrn* (Neukirchen-Vluyn 1987) esp. 107ff.

17. See J. Moltmann *Diakonie im Horizont des Reiches Gottes* (Neukirchen-Vluyn 1984) 36.

18. For more detail on this see J. Moltmann, loc. cit. esp. 22–41. 52–73. See also F. Kamphaus *Die Wahrheit in Liebe tun*. On the status of Caritas in the parish, in P. Nordhues et al (Pub.) *Handbuch der Caritasarbeit* (Paderborn 1986) 513–525; R. Weth 'Diakonie' in:' Chr. Bäumler/N. Mette (Pub.) *Gemeindepraxis in Grundbegriffen* (Munich-Duesseldorf 1987) 116–126; H. Stainkamp loc. cit.; H. Theurich loc. cit.

19. J. Degen 'Diakonische Competenz der Gemeinde vor Ort' unpublished manuscript, 17.

20. R. Weth loc. cit. 121f.

Elisabeth Schüssler Fiorenza

'Waiting at Table': A Critical Feminist Theological Reflection on Diakonia

THE GREEK term *diakonia* means literally 'waiting at tables' but is usually translated as 'service' or 'ministry'.[1] We can distinguish two different meanings in the New Testament usage of the word-cluster *diakonia/diakonos/diakonein* which have become paradigmatic for later theology. In a religious-spiritualised sense the word-cluster signifies a honorary activity, a person standing in the service of God/s, in the service of a city or commonwealth or in the service of great ideas or ideals. When used in the New Testament in this sense the word-cluster characterises Christian preachers and missionaries like Paul or Phoebe as representatives and messengers of God.

However, in its original sense the term means actual material service, waiting at table and other menial tasks. The 'servant' had a low social position, was dependent on her or his master/mistress and could not command respect. However, despite the debasing negative social connotations of its original meaning 'service' has become the key-symbol for the revival of a 'servant ecclesiology' with progressive intentions. Feminist theological attempts to salvage this biblical symbol in the face of the stringent feminist critique of its cultural-political function in the oppression of women share the assumption of such a 'servant ecclesiology', that self-sacrificing 'service' is central to Christian identity and community.

1. SERVANT ECCLESIOLOGY AND WOMEN'S MINISTRY

Since the early sixties the image of the servant-church has to come to dominate progressive Roman Catholic and Protestant ecclesiologies and ministerial self-understanding. This revival of a theology of *diakonia* went hand in hand with a change in the Church's attitude to the 'world'. For instance the Pastoral Constitution on the Church in the Modern World of Vatican II teaches in Article 3, that just as Jesus Christ became human not to be served but to serve so also the Church seeks to serve the world by fostering 'the brotherhood of all men'. In his book *Models of the Church*, Avery Dulles points out that a similar servant ecclesiology motivates official statements of other churches:

> 'Remarkable in this respect are the Presbyterian Confession of 1967, the Uppsala Report of the World Council of Churches in 1968, the Conclusion of the Second General Conference of Latin American Bishops at Medellin in 1968, and the document on Justice in the World issued by the Roman Catholic Synod of Bishops at its fall meeting in 1971.[2]

Such a servant ecclesiology insists with Bonhoeffer 'that the Church is the Church only when it exists for others'.[3] In so far as this theology does not critically analyse the social underpinnings of servant-langage it is not able to recognise it as 'theological double-speak' since the theology of service has different implications for men and women, ordained and non-ordained, powerful and powerless.

This servant ecclesiology legitimates a diversification of 'ministry' in the Roman Catholic context. Its theologians argue that ministries are functional, that they are a specific gift and service to the community. They exist for the building up of the community and do not consist in special status, lifestyle, or sacred office. Since the servant Church as the ministerial community is prior to its ministers,[4] the Church can officially sanction new ministries that complement the traditional hierarchical ministries of bishop, priest and deacon.[5] Thus this theology does not seriously challenge the Church's structures of patriarchal hierarchy and the 'class' division between ordained and non-ordained ministries but exhorts those who have patriarchal clerical status and ecclesiastical powers to serve the laity and those in need.

In Roman Catholicism this ecclesiology was developed in response to the shortage of priests in many parts of the world. It has engendered an explosion of specialised ministries that seek to serve not only the needs of the Church but also those of the world. It has allowed women to exercise ministerial functions, even though the official stance against the inclusion of women in the ordained ministry has increasingly hardened. In short, the 'progressive' theology of ministry as service as well as of the Church as the servant of the world has supported not only a variety of ministries but also the participation of women in the ministry of the Church.[6]

However because of their gender women are relegated by law to subservient tasks, auxiliary roles, and secondary status in ministry, since according to Canon Law only those in orders can receive jurisdiction (the power of decision-making) and are entitled to officially exercise sacramental powers. While the Vatican has acknowledged that the majority of people in evangelisation are women,[7] a US study on women in ministry has documented that most women in ministry do unpaid volunteer work—or are minimally paid if they are remunerated at all. Women engaged in such volunteer ministry are mostly middle-aged, middle-class married women whose children have left the home, who have no professional career, and whose husbands are able to support them. At the price of their continuing economic dependence they can 'afford' ministry, whereas poor women and welfare mothers are not able to do so. The 'double-speak of ministry' is illustrated by this study, in so far as men exercise ministry by virtue of ordination, whereas women render ministry only when they do not receive financial, social or professional gains.[8]

At the same time this servant ecclesiology has motivated women to acquiesce to their 'second class' ministerial status and prevented us from insisting on our rights as church-workers. Several years ago I met with a group of pastoral assistants in Würzburg who complained that as women they are not allowed to preach whereas permanent deacons were able to do so although they had much less theological education and pastoral experience. When it was suggested that all the pastoral assistants in the city should 'go on strike' in protest against such blatant discrimination, the women were horrified because—as one of them put it—they had dedicated their life to the service of the Church.

Such subservient and secondary ministerial status of women is also found in Christian churches that ordain women.[9] Governing boards and decision-making positions are often restricted to male clergy. Women clergy are not seldom relegated to small rural parishes, are paid less than men with comparable qualifications and remain at the level of assistant ministers. At the same time clergywomen are, as ordained professionals, better off than other female church workers and volunteer-staff. In the churches as in society at large the majority of social-charitable volunteer workers are women.[10] The servanthood of the Church thus seems to be represented by women.

In a ministerial situation of institutional inequality, the theology of ministry as service and its underlying servant ecclesiology serve to internalise and legitimate the patriarchal-hierarchical status quo in theological-spiritual terms. Despite of its progressive intentions a servant-ecclesiology reproduces the assymetric dualism between Church and world, clergy and laity, religious and secular, men and women that is generated by patriarchal-hierarchical church structures. In so far as ecclesial relationships are structured and conceptualised in such a way that the church, clergy, religious, and men remain still the defining subjects, a servant ecclesiology rhetorically claims service and servanthood for those who have patriarchal-hierarchical status and exercise spiritual power and control. For instance, the 'Holy Father' has supreme authority and power in the Roman Catholic church but is at the same time called *servus servorum dei*, the 'servant of God's servants'. However as long as actual power relationships and status privileges are not changed such a servant rhetoric must remain a mere moralistic sentiment and appeal that mystifies structures of domination.

2. CULTURAL CONTEXT AND FUNCTION

Such a theology of servanthood becomes even more questionable when its cultural-social contexts come into view. In Western cultures women are socialised to self-less love in order to perform upaid services in the family as well as volunteer services in the public domain. The myth of 'true womanhood', romantic love, and domesticity defines women's nature as 'being for others', and women's identity as derived from husband and children. Women are expected to give up their names, their careers, and their possessions for the well-being of their families and for the sake of 'personal relationships'. Especially mothers are to sacrifice their life in the service of their children and all those in need.

Whereas men are socialised into masculine roles of self-assertion, independence and control, women are socialised to self-denial, self-abnegation and self-sacrifice in the service of others. Our sin is the failure to become a self.[11] This cultural socialisation of women to self-less femininity and altruistic behaviour is reinforced and perpetated by the Christian preaching of self-sacrificing love and self-denying service. Since Jesus Christ humbled himself and sacrificed his life for the salvation of others, the notion of self-sacrificing love and humble service is at the heart of Christian ethics. Not only Christ, the perfect servant and sacrifice of God but also Mary, the obedient handmaid of God are the models of true Christian womanhood.

However, this Christian theology of service must be scrutinised not only for its cultural androcentric presuppositions and implications. It must also be analysed with respect to its classist, racist, and colonialist underpinnings. Beginning with Plato and Aristotle, Western political philosophy has argued that the freeborn, propertied, educated man is the highest of mortal beings and that all other members of the human race are defined by their functions in his service. Women as well as slaves and barbarians are by 'nature' inferior to him and therefore destined to be the instruments of his well-being.[12] Modern political and philosophical anthropology continues to assume that propertied, educated 'White Western Man' is defined by reason, self-determination, and full citizenship whereas women and other subordinated peoples are characterised by emotion, service and dependence.[13] They are seen not as rational and responsible but as emotional and child-like.

In short, patriarchal society and culture is not only characterised by its sexual and economic exploitation of all women which is sustained and legitimised by the cult of true womanhood, the myth of femininity, romantic love, and edcation to domesticity.[14] It also needs for its functioning a 'servant class', a 'servant race,' or a 'servant people', be they slaves, serfs, house servants, coolies or mammies. The existence of such a 'servant class' is maintained through law, education, socialisation, and brute violence. It is sustained by the belief that members of a 'servant class' of people are by nature or by divine decree inferior to those whom they are destined to serve.[15]

Moreover, the cultural 'hierarchy of service' implicates women in the exploitation of other women. True, even the noble lady of the castle or the white lady of the plantation was to be subservient to her father or husband as the 'lord and master of the house.' Yet she was able to delegate her labours to a 'servant group' of people, especially to impoverished, uneducated, and colonialised women.[16] The cultural assumption of all women's sexual and domestic subservience to the 'Man' thus pits women against women in a patriarchal society in so far as women have to control and supervise the low-paid domestic service and work of other women. The more the economic power of working- and middle-class male salaries erodes, women of these economic strata also have increasingly to shoulder the triple burden of unpaid housework, care of children as well as of the elderly and infirm, and work outside the home.[17] Lower class, Black and Hispanic women workers always had to do so.

Finally, the increase of virulent right-wing ideologies in the past decade,— such as racism, antisemitism, 'work-fare' programmes for the poor, biblicist fundamentalism, militarist colonialism and 'the new cult of femininity and the family'—seek to maintain the servanthood of exploited people by insisting that by the will of God or by 'nature' some groups of people are superior and others subservient. The renewed ecclesiastical insistence that women must live their true womanhood in complementarity with men as well as that the ordained differ 'in essence' from the laity, must be seen in this context. As Letty Russell so succinctly states:

'Regardless of what we say about ministry as a function, we [the clergy] are still placed in a position of permanent superiority in the life of the Church.

In this sense ordination becomes an indelible mark of caste rather than the recognition of spiritual gifts for a particular ministry in the Church.'[18]

The theological langage of ordained ministry as servant leadership does not abolish the ecclesial 'class' division between clergy and laity but mystifies and perpetrates it.

3. SERVANTHOOD ECCLESIOLOGY IN FEMINIST THEOLOGY

However, in spite of the feminist critique of the cultural and religious socialisation of women and other subordinated peoples to self-sacrificing love and self-less service for others, the notion of ministry as service is still a powerful symbol for Christian feminists. Some have argued that 'as Christians we cannot avoid the word, despite of its oppressive overtones', since *diakonia* is central to the understanding of the mission and ministry of Christ as well as to that of the Church.[19] Such a feminist theological retrieval of a servanthood-ecclesiology basically follows two strategies of interpretation.

The first, strategy elaborates the New Testament distinction between *diakonein* and *douleuein* in order to stress that freely chosen service means liberation. *Diakonia*-service is to be differentiated from servility. Servanthood without choice is not *diakonia* but becomes slavery (*douleia*). However, 'servanthood through choice is an act of the total self. The powerlessness of servanthood can be redemptive only when it results from free and conscious choice'. Such freely chosen servanthood is not self-denial, self-elimination, self-ignorance or self-immolation. Rather it is the 'capacity to look beyond ourselves to see the needs of others'. It is the 'empathy to want to help and the skill to know how to help'.

Jesus is the model of such freely chosen service because he has made choices of self-giving and self-sacrifice rather than allowing society to dictate his behaviour. *Diakonia* is realised in the life of Jesus who came 'not to be served but to serve and to give his life as ransom for many' (Mark 10:45). If 'servanthood is being in love with the world as God is in love with it', then servanthood means, in the last analysis, liberation. 'We find ourselves liberated into servanthood.'[20] However this feminist proposal for the theological recuperation of servanthood does not take into account that people who in a patriarchal culture and church are powerless, singled out and socialised into subservience and a life of servanthood are not able 'to choose freely' servanthood.

By re-valorising service and servanthood theologically this strategy extends the theological 'double-speak' about service to the theological concept of liberation. For those who are destined by patriarchal culture and socio-political structures to become 'servants' to those who have power over them, the theological or ecclesiological retrieval of 'service/servant/slave/waiter' language cannot have a liberating function as long as patriarchal structres in society and Church continue to divide people into those who serve and those who are served. Rather than elaborate the theological symbols of service/servitude/and self-sacrifice a critical feminist theology of liberation instead must seek for New Testament concepts such as e.g., *dynamis/exousia/soteria* (power/authority/and well-being) that can critically challenge the religious reproduction of a cultural servant mentality.

A second feminist theological strategy for retrieving the theology of service does not so much focus on the freely chosen integration of women's cultural and Christian socialisation for self-less service and love but concentrates on a redefinition of ministry. By combining the theology of 'freely chosen' service with an understanding of ministry not as 'power over' but as 'power for', it seeks to recover the early Christian understanding of ministry as service of God and as the building up of the community. It also takes Jesus Christ and his incarnation as 'suffering servant' as the model of Christian ministry:

> Diakonia is kenotic or self-emptying of power as domination. Ministry transforms power from power over others to empowerment of others. The abdication of power as domination has nothing to do with servility ... Rather ministry means exercising power in a new way, as a means of liberation of one another.[21]

Although this reconceptualisation of ministry seeks to retrieve the New Testament model of *diakonia* = service for a feminist ecclesial self-understanding in and through a redefinition of power, it nevertheless valorises the patriarchal concept and institution of service/servanthood theologically. The theological language of ministry as service i.e., as 'power for' rather than as 'power over' the Church and the world obfuscates the fact that the patriarchal church continues to exercise its ministry as 'power over.' It remains structured into a hierarchy of power dualisms: ordained/non-ordained, clergy/laity, religious/secular, Church/world.

Continuing to use the theological notion of service as a central feminist category for ministry, this theology of service reduplicates the cultural pattern of self-sacrificing service for women and other subordinate peoples, while at the same time continuing to serve as a moralistic appeal to those who have positions of power and control in church leadership. Dependence, obedience, second class citizenship and powerlessness remain intrinsic to the notion of 'service/servanthood' as long as society and Church structurally reproduce a 'servant' class of people. Therefore, in seeking to define women's ministry a feminist ecclesiology of liberation must reject the categories of service and servanthood as disempowering to women. New Testament categories for ecclesial leadership functions such as e.g., apostles, prophets, facilitators, missionary co-workers and co-laborators dedicated to the *oikodome* i.e., 'the building up of the community' would be more appropriate to express a feminist understanding of ministry as empowerment.

It must therefore be asked whether the New Testament notion of diakonia as service should be completely discarded by feminists. I would suggest that the notion of diakonia can be reclaimed by feminist theology solely as a critical category challenging those who have actual power and privilege in patriarchal Church and society. Since oppressions are interstructured, hierarchised and multi-faceted, women who do not live on the bottom of the patriarchal pyramid are not only exploited but they also benefit from the structures of domination and service. Those of us who are marginalised and subordinated but at the same time privileged either by virtue of ordination, education, wealth, nationality, race, health or age have to use our privileges for bringing about change. Feminist ministers do not seek to be incorporated into the lowest ranks of the patriarchal hierarchy as altar-servers, lectors, deaconesses or even priests but engage in ministry in order to subvert clerical-hierarchal structures and to transform the patriarchal Church into a discipleship of equals.

Such a retrieval of diakonia for a critical challenge to the structures of domination corresponds to its meaning in the gospel traditions. The core saying of Mark 10:42–44 which in some form is assumed to go back to the historical Jesus, juxtaposes 'great/servant' and 'first/slave'. The subject under discussion is the contrast between societal structures of domination and the 'discipleship of equals'.[22] It clearly presupposes a society in which those who 'rule and have authority over' are the kings and great ones, whereas those who are servants and slaves are required to take orders, to render obeisance and provide services. It challenges those in positions of dominance and power to become 'equal' with those who are powerless. Masters should relinquish domination over their slaves and servants and step into their shoes.

The importance of this saying is indicated by its inclusion in the synoptic tradition in a seven-fold combination (Mark 10:42–45 par. Matt. 20:25–27; 23:11; Luke 22:26; Mark 9:33–37 par. Matt. 18:1–4; Luke 9:48). Its meaning is also central to the Fourth Gospel (John 12:25–26 and 13:4–5.12–17). This Jesus-tradition does not exhort all Christians to become servants and slaves but only those who have status and power in the patriarchal pyramid. It seeks to create 'equality from below' not by incorporating those on the bottom of the patriarchal pyramid into its lower ranks. Rather it rejects the patriarchal-hierarchical pyramid as such. It seeks to level it in by calling those on the top of the pyramid to join the work and labour of those on the bottom thereby making a 'servant class' of people superfluous. By denying the validity of master and lord positions and by ironically calling the 'would-be' great and leaders to live on the bottom of the patriarchal pyramid of domination, this Jesus-tradition paradoxically rejects all patriarchal-hierarchical structures and positions.

The ecclesial process of interpretation in the gospels applied a saying originally addressed to the whole people of Israel to its own community structures and relationships. Structures of domination and servanthood should not be tolerated in the community of equals. True leadership in the community must be rooted in solidarity with each other. This ecclesial process of interpretation takes place at the same time when the post-Pauline traditions in the interest of 'good citizenship' advocate the adaptation of the Christian community as 'the household of God' to its patriarchal societal structures. This patriarchalising tendency also had impact on the interpretation of diakonia in the gospels.

Whereas Mark and Matthew acknowledge no 'great' and 'first' in the community at all, Luke does so. His only requirement is that their style of leadership orientate itself on the example of Jesus. Like Luke and the post-Pauline tradition later theologians have no longer understood the radical paradox of the discipleship of equals when they called those in positions of wealth and power to 'charitable service'. This theology of service did not question but confirmed patriarchal status and privileges. Since it has defined main-line Christian self-understanding and community and has condoned structures of 'domination and authority over', a feminist theology of ministry must deconstruct such patriarchal Christian self-understandings and ecclesial structures and not perpetuate it by valorising the notion of service and servanthood. Ministry is no longer to be construed as 'service' or as 'waiting on someone' but should be understood as 'equality from below' in solidarity with all those who struggle for survival, self-love and justice.

Notes

1. See H. W. Beyer '*diakoneo*' *Theological Dictionary of the New Testament*, Vol. II, pp. 81–93; K. H. Rengstorf, '*doulos*,' *ibid.* pp. 261–280; K. H. Hess 'serve' *New International Dictionary of New Testament Theoplogy*, Vol. III, pp. 544–549; R. Tuente 'slave' *ibid.*, pp. 592–598.

2. Avery Dulles *Models of the Church* (Garden City 1974) p. 87. See also J. E. Booty *The Servant Church* (Wilton 1984).

3.   D. Bonhöffer *Letters and Papers from Prison* (rev. ed.New York 1967) p. 203.

4. See e.g., E. Schillebeeckx *Ministry: Leadership in the Community of Jesus Christ* (New York 1982) p. 147; D. Power *Gifts that Differ: Lay Ministries Established and Unestablished* (New York 1980) p. 106.

5. See J. A. Coleman 'A Theology of Ministry' *The Way* 25 (1985) pp. 15–17 with reference to P. Chirico 'Pastoral Ministry in a Time of Priest Shortage' *The Clergy Review* 69 (1984) pp. 81–84.

6. The first list of proposals made by the 1987 Synod on the Laity contained the following recommendation which reflected the mind of the Synod:

'Because of the fundamental equal dignity of the disciples of Christ, all offices and tasks in the Church except the ministries which require the power of orders should be open to women as well as men, with due regard to local sensibilities.'

However, this and the recommendations to study the admission of women to the ministry of deaconesses as well as to that of 'altar-servers' disappeared without any convincing explanation from the subsequent drafts. See P. Hebblethwaite, 'Reports Reveal Curia Derailed Lay Synod' *National Catholic Reporter* 24 (5 February 1988) p. 28.

7. 'The Role of Women in Evangelization' issued by the Pastoral Commission of the Vatican Congregation for the Evangelisation of Peoples. The text can be found in *Origins* 5 (April 1976) 702–707.

8. *Women and Ministry: A Survey of the Experience of Roman Catholic Women in the United States* (Washington 1980). See my analysis of this study: 'We Are Still Invisible. Theological Analysis of "Women and Ministry"' in D.Gottemoeller and R. Hofbauer (eds.) *Women and Ministry: Present Experience and Future Hope* (Washington 1981) 29–43.

9. See J. W. Carroll, B. Hargrove, A. Lummis *Women of the Cloth* (San Francisco 1983); J. L. Weidman (ed.) *Women Ministers* (San Francisco 1981); A. Schilthuis-Stokvis 'Women as Workers in the Church Seen from the Ecumenical Point of View' *Concilium* 194 (1987) 85–90.

10. See e.g., G. Notz 'Frauenarbeit zum Nulltarif. Zur ehrenamtlichen Tätigkeit von Frauen' in Arbeitsgemeinschaft Frauenforschung der Universität Bonn, *Studium Feminale* (Bonn 1986) 134–151.

11. See Judith Plaskow *Sex, Sin and Grace* (Washington 1980).

12. Susan Moller Okin *Women in Western Political Thought* (Princeton 1979) 73–96.

13. See Elisabeth List 'Homo Politicus—Femina Privata. Thesen zur Kritik der politischen Anthropologie' in J. Conrad and U. Konnertz *Weiblichkeit in der Moderne. Ansätze feministischer Vernunftkritik* (Tübingen 1986) 75–95.

14. See Brigitte Weisshaupt 'Selbstlosigkeit und Wissen' in *Weiblichkeit in der Moderne* pp. 21–38.

15. See e.g., the biographical reflection and analysis of apartheid as an ideology and institution for maintaining a 'servant people' by Mark Mathabene *Kaffir Boy. The True Story of a Black Youth's Coming Of Age in Apartheid South Africa* (New York 1986).

16. See e.g., Martha Mamozai *Herrenmenschen. Frauen im deutschen Kolonialismus* (rororo 4959; Rheinbeck 1982).

17. See the contributions in E. Schüssler Fiorenza and A. Carr (ed.) *Women, Work, and Poverty*, Concilium 194 (Edinburgh 1987).

18. Letty M. Russell 'Women and Ministry: Problem or Possibility?' in J. L. Weidman (ed.) *Christian Feminism—Visions of a New Humanity* (San Francisco 1984) p. 89.

19. Letty M. Russell 'Women and Ministry' in A. L. Hageman *Sexist Religion and Women in the Church* (New York 1974) pp. 55ff.

20. All quotations are taken from R. Richardson Smith 'Liberating the Servant' *The Christian Century* 98 (1981) p. 1314; see also R. Propst 'Servanthood Redefined: Coping Mechanism for Women Within Protestant Christianity' *Journal of Pastoral Counseling* 17 (1982) 14–18.

21. R. Radford Ruether *Sexism and God-Talk. Toward a Feminist Theology* (Boston 1983) p. 207; See also the various contributions of Letty M. Russell.

22. For the following see my book *In Memory of Her. A Feminist Theological Reconstruction of Christian Origins* (New York 1983) pp. 148–151.

Patrick Kalilombe

Diakonia in Universal Context: An African Point of View

'If one of you wants to be great, he must be the servant (*diakonos*) of the rest; and if one of you wants to be first, he must be the slave (*doulos*) of all. For even the Son of Man did not come to be served (*diakonēthēnai*); he came to serve (*diakonēsai*) and to give his life to redeem many people'. Mark 10:43–45

THE LANGUAGE of *diakonia* or service is not as straightforward as it might sound to most of us accustomed to the usual sacral parlance of the Church. The emotional connotations it evokes are ambiguous. They can be positive and reassuring, but also negative and depressing. It all depends on who is talking. In Church context, 'Divine Service', deacon and diaconate, are positive images of service the Lord 'to serve whom is to reign'. In the same way the priest or pastor refers with humble gratitude to the congregation he 'serves', and feels it is an honour to be the 'servant' of God's people. The missionary too will describe how he 'served' in such or such a place. Even in secular society there are 'ministers' and civil 'servants'; soldiers are proud of their military 'service', just as colonial officrs used to recall nostalgically how they 'served' here or there in various capacities.

But there are other people for whom service is a painful experience. The prisoner who 'serves' a life sentence, the maid—'servant' rising early and going to bed late after a hard long day: for these, 'service' is neither romantic nor enjoyable. Nor does the poor nation, obliged to 'service' its growing debts, find the idea of diakonia particularly thrilling. All these are on the painful side of the service relationship. Their experience warns us that the topic of service is complex and confusing. Especially today, its discussion forces us to look into harsh realities and to ask rather embarrassing questions about the nature and dynamics of the various services which we expect from one another. The Church itself must ask whether and in what ways its claim to be at the service of the world makes sense.

Service is never one-sided: it implies mutuality. It assumes that there are needs on one side, to satisfy which the help of the other side is required. Thus, one side gives and another receives. This is a demonstration of an elementary truth of life: nobody is an island; we all need one another since we belong together. Peace, well-being, development and prosperity depend on a whole complex network of exchanges: giving and receiving goods and services in complementary ways. As individuals and as communities, we are basically inter-dependent.

It seems opportune today to take a good honest look at service. The spectacle of more and more people in our world becoming poorer and poorer, whole nations going down in desperate misery and lacking even the bare necessities of life in a world which could easily offer a decent life to every one— that spectacle is a clear enough proof that the functioning of mutual service has somehow broken down. Africa, for example, is currently drawing our attention because of its growing pockets of misery: chronic famines, endless conflicts which generate millions of refugees, dislocation of national economies producing unemployment, galloping inflation, debased currencies, and dire want, while meagre resources are diverted to buy arms. Something is surely wrong in the functioning of services, not only locally but also on the global scale. And Africa is not alone in this. Vast areas of Asia and Latin America are in a similar plight. Even in the so-called affluent nations, there are growing areas of poverty and deprivation. In the midst of it all, what evidence is there that the Church is indeed a servant Church? Are there proofs that it is showing the way towards a hopeful change when mutual service and sensitivity to one another's needs will be the guiding tenets?

It would be tempting to answer such questions rather optimistically or in an apologetic and self-justifying way. We might want, for example, to grant that of late there have been signs of a cooling down in the Church's serving spirit. Some would see as a sign in this sense the dramatic fall in 'vocations' within those sectors of the Church where service used to be demonstrated in the most convincing way, for example, in missionary orders, in the ordained ministry, and in religious congregations of both men and women. Others might go a step farther and admit that in countries where poverty, oppression, exploitation, and the violation of human rights are most obvious, as is the case in many areas of the Third World, the Church is not always on the side of the suffering masses. Often leaders—bishops, priests, religious, and prominent lay people—seem to go along with the structures and powers responsible for these evils. Or at least they do not exhibit any particular sensitivity for the poor and the oppressed. This kind of judgment—however justified in some cases—runs the risk of being too general, and in any case it hardly begins to answer the real question: how is that possible in a so-called servant church? Moreover one oc7ld easily answer by recalling that in the past decade Church authorities, from as high up as the Pope himself down to episcopal conferences in all parts of the world, have solemnly committed the Church to 'siding with the poor and the oppressed'. These declarations are not empty words.

And yet, judging by present tragic developments, this siding with the poor does not seem to make much difference. The Church may indeed be making laudable efforts to be at the service of the underprivileged. But many of those who are on the suffering side would find it hard to say what change this concern for them has made in their lot. Is there, then, something else that needs to be done?

1. LOOKING AT 'SERVICE' FROM THE UNDERSIDE OF HISTORY

It is just possible that the whole question needs to be looked at from an angle different from the usual one. When service is being discussed and planned for, it is usually from the side of those who are in a position to come to the aid of the needy. In other words, the vision is from the side of the better off and the more powerful. There is nothing really wrong with that. But still, it must be admitted that from that angle, only part of the reality is visible. There may be many crucial aspects which remain hidden and are not taken seriously into account in the understanding of the facts or in the formulation of projects which such an understanding suggests.

These days we are beginning to realise more and more that our understanding of and dealing with realities depends very much on where we are. Some years ago, for example, it used to be taken for granted that there was only one, universally valid, theology since objective reality, objective truth, can only be one. But today there is a growing acceptance of pluralism in theological thought and formulation. We have liberation theologies, feminist theologies, African, Asian, and other theologies. When talk about objective truth comes up, the question is: objective for whom? The sophism behind the claim about one (or universal) theology lies in a confusion between the one absolute Word of God on the one side and the human reflections on it on the other.

Since theology is critical reflection on the Word of God, there is bound to be a variety of such reflections depending on who does the reflection and the angles from which such reflection is done. The point is not really whether or not there can be different or conflicting truths, but whether any truth at all can be fully arrived at from just one point of view. About the questions themselves that are deemed worth investigating, we need to ask: why are those questions important rather than some others? For whom are they important? And why? Then comes the problem of priorities: which question is more important among the several possible ones? Who decides that? What happens when that decision is made? Who gains from it? In other words, there is a concrete human background which bears on the actual shape of the reflection.

At any rate one suspects that the question of diakonia would gain in intelligibility if, for a change, it were seen from another angle. If service has usually been visualised from the side of those who can afford to serve others, it is perhaps time to look at it from the viewpoint of those who are served. How do *they* see this service? How does it feel to be the object of other people's benefaction? Have they any suggestions or questions? In the course of this (1987) year's 'One World Week' in Britain, the topic of which was: 'Who gets the Credit?', I had the feeling that people in the poor countries were asking three types of questions: What do you mean service: who is serving whom? In what spirit is this service being done? What is the real objective of this service?

These reflections on service are being made from the point of view of an African, taking into account not only the present situation but also the long past history of the continent. Although the main focus is understandably that of the Christian Church's involvement with African realities, and therefore primarily concerned with spiritual matters, we include the wider impact of the Western world generally. Therefore concerns of a more worldy nature will come in, such as political, economic, social and cultural interactions. The reason is simple. Historically Christian evangelisation came to Africa at the same time that European and American peoples were penetrating the continent. However different their aims may have been, they shared a common sense of mission towards Africa: they all came to accomplish some sort of service. It is this general idea of service that will be the object of examination. The religious and the secular understanding of service may have been different, but there was much in common between them, at least from the point of view of the Africans.

Back home in Africa, I often pondered on the connotations put into a word which serves to designate potentially all those who come to us from Europe and America, whether missionaries or secular agents: *Mzungu* (pl. *azungu*). this word, I discovered, could be used in two different ways. In a simple and general way, it means 'white people'. But then there is more to the word than mere colour or race. It denotes also an attitude, a way of relating to other people, a way of acting and reacting. 'Mzungu' is: (1) somebody irremediably convinced of being superior to others, and therefore expecting to be treated as such; (2) someone who usually acts for selfish purposes even when doing good; (3) a person who, in dealing with others, uses exploitative methods.

Mzungu is by no means a purely racial attribute. The proof is that black Africans will call fellow blacks 'azungu akuda' (black azungu) if they demonstrate the three characteristics. On the other hand there are cases in which people will say of a European: 'He does not act like mzungu'! But it is clear that historically the mzungu model arose from bitter experiences with generations of expatriates.

My basic contention is that when service is rendered in a *mzungu* way, it ultimately ceases to be true service. The reason why much that passes for service is not regarded as such by those who are supposed to be the beneficiaries, maybe because they just provide for the interests of those who serve, or finally because they do not liberate or empower the needy, but maintain them in a state of dependence. If the Church is to promote true service in our world, here is a whole programme for examination and action.

2. WHAT IS SERVICE? WHO SERVES WHOM?

For ages Africa has been considered a continent that needed help. This Dark Continent, rich in natural resources, and yet inhabited by primitive tribes whom civilization and progress had bypassed, and among whom the knowledge of the true God was thought to be absent, attracted many outsiders. Some of these came wth simple, straightforward objectives of plunder and exploitation. They seemed to think they were coming into a no-man's land: the rights of the inhabitants (the 'natives', 'indigenous people') were non-existent or could be brushed aside with impunity. But the majority did take into account the presence of local people. Such in-comers felt the need to justify their coming. It was usually in terms of a sort of service. The general explanation was that they came to share with the natives the benefits of civilization: to help them develop and make progress. Christian evangelists came to teach about God, to preach Jesus Christ, to save souls, or to bring in true religion.

The idea of coming to Africa to help those in need is still very much alive. It was there during the years of colonialism. Even after independence there have been many aid projects, development plans, trade missions, education and technical assistance organisations, through which the industrialised antions have been at the service of Africa. There is no denying that much good has been done.

But the question is: Through all this, who is being served really? Who is getting the meaningful benefit from these relationships? Recent studies, such as Guy Arnold's *Aid and the Third World: the North/South Divide* (London: Robert Royce, 1985), seem to demonstrate that services purportedly being offered to the poor nations end up often becoming a way whereby the poor actually serve the rich. The donor is finally the recipient, while the original recipient is left much the loser. This is because the one truly consistent law in such services is that they will serve the interests of the donor nations. At the heart of the transaction is the objective of profit: self-interest.

For the Church, inter-dependence and mutual concern are a necessary consequence of its message of love. It is its duty therefore to expose and denounce the ruthless exploitative practices of nations and business concerns which often hide behind the pretence of helping the poor. But mere pious pronouncements are not enough. What is needed is a clear demonstration through acts of engagement, whereby the Church dissociates itself from these practices, accepts incurring the wrath of prsons and bodies (often its own faithful and supporting members) which want it to keep out of politics, economics or social concerns and stick to its so-called religious sphere. The Church should be prepared to pay the price of being isolated, victimised and punished for its stance, as when benefactors of its undertaking with draw their support and suppress the privileges they used to give the Church. A gesture such as withdrawing investments (however advantageous) from a bank or company practising exploitation is a risky gamble. But only at the price of such risks can the Church witness convincingly to the service of the poor.

3. IN WHAT SPIRIT IS SERVICE BEING DONE?

A basic mzungu characteristic is a complex of superiority. In relations with other people the mzungu insists being on the upper hand, in a position to dictate conditions and control what is going on. Competition rather than co-operation on an equal footing. When services are undertaken, there is always a basic requirement that one side is to dominate. In history there have been clear cases of unequal treaties; colonialism was based on precisely such agreements. If we look at modern political, military, or trade agreements we shall find that the same pattern prevails. One needs only to think of the UN CTAD meetings or the working of the International Monetary Fund. Quite naturally the interest of the dominated or inferior partner are seen only in function of the interests of the dominant powers; and that is why the poor nations are always on the losing side.

Here again the Church should be able to propose a different model, that of Jesus Christ. Paul enjoins the believers to 'look out for one another's interests, not just for your own. The attitude you should have is the one that Christ Jesus had ... Of his own free will he gave up all he had, and took the nature of a servant' (Phil. 2:4–5,7). Service is genuine and effective if it is accompanied by an attitude of humility. Concretely speaking, true service demands that each side, the one serving and the one being served, does not seek advantages over the other, but accept each other as partners in a common mutual service.

Our world today, divided unfairly between the powerful North and the poor South, is in need of conversion. It needs to learn what mutual service means and demands in this inter-dependent global village. The Church proclaims the message of the true Servant of God who came not to be served but to serve and give his life for the multitude. But the Church can proclaim this message with power only if it practises convincingly this type of costly service. Perhaps the conversion which is required will come more easily if the Church learns to listen to the poor and the powerless, the frustrated objects of false services. Their forced service in the interests of the wealthy and the powerful will hopefully lend force to Christ's own prescription: *Not to be served but to serve.*

Johannes Degen

Diakonia as an Agency in the Welfare State

1. THE SCOPE AND STRUCTURE OF DIAKONIA IN THE FEDERAL REPUBLIC OF GERMANY

THE DEVELOPED welfare state of the Federal German Republic would not be what it is without the contribution made by Christian social agenices closely connected with the Evangelical Church in Germany. At national level the 17,873 institutions employing 163,405 full time and 62,686 part time personnel (as at 1 January 1984) are one of the most influential among the five non-governmental welfare agencies involved in the public social services. Appreciably more than half of the full-time workers, and also of the part time ones, is employed in hospitals and in youth-oriented services.

The statistics both of the Evangelical Church in Germany and of its joint social service agency the Diakonische Werk show the strikingly high total of 7,112 kindergartens, day nurseries and schools employing 23,674 full time and 14,366 part time workers. Besides the institutions, self-help groups, groups of helpers and clubs not connected with social service institutions have been set up in the recent past. Some 4,836 groups of this kind are at present functioning under the aegis of the diakonia of the church.

These agencies, which form part of the total non-governmental effort in this sphere, are supplemented by the public social services. It is difficult to say what proportion of the total social service system the Evangelical Church's contribution represents; it differs widely in different spheres of social work. Certainly it is comparatively strongly represented in hospitals and in work among young, old and handicapped people, so far as the non-governmental agencies are concerned. Without claiming completeness, we should like to refer to some problems in regard to the structure of the diaconal work-force. The year 1975 was the last in which the Evangelical Church in Germany and the joint social agencies attempted a joint census of their workers and helpers. At that time it became apparent that of the total of those employed in Church and diakonia, 2/3 were in the latter and 1/3 in the former. In 1975, 32.3 per cent of the employees working in the Church's social services were employed by a church organisation and 67.7 per cent by an independent organisation. These figures justify the broad generalisation that a considerable proportion of the people serving in the diakonia are working outside the church (as a public law corporation). If welfare agencies as constituents of the total welfare activities of society occupy an intermediate place between the formal sectors of market and state bureaucracy on the one hand and the informal units (the primary groups), this naturally applies to the diakonia as well. But in their case a further distinction has to be made—they occupy an intermediate place between the church organisation and a social service.

Indeed, this intermediate position of diakonia between the church and the social services is evident form the way in which they are financed. In 1980 the operating costs of all the Church's social agencies in West Germany amounted to DM 794,000 million. Of this sum the State contributed 38 per cent, compulsory insurance covered 34 per cent, and 11 per cent was found internally, most of it coming from the Church's budget. Capital expenditure amounts to some DM 400 million annually, of which about 15 per cent is met by loans and grants from the Church, whilst the State bears 45 per cent of the capital investment costs. If we look at the way in which the kindergartens run by the Evangelical Church in Germany were financed in 1979 we find that nationwide an averge 25.2 per cent for this diaconal work was contributed by the 17 member churches from their own funds, despite very wide differences in the financial treatment of this service in the various provinces of West Germany. In 1979 alone, DM 943 million were contributed for kindergarten work out of a total of DM 7,200 million collected by the Evangelical Church in Germany and its associated churches.

By reason both of their history and of their present status under the national laws affecting the Church. The social agencies of the Church in West Germany regard themselves as part of the Church's field of action, and an essential constitutive part of the Church. But viewed as institutions they also take the form of a welfare agency and as such they also obey imperatives other than specifically ecclesiastical ones. Legally they have to comply with rules laid down both by the Church and the State. They are financed jointly by the Church, the insurance companies and the State, and because of this they have to bear in mind, in their theory and practice, that at the present time this area of the Church's operations is the most complex field of interaction between Church and society.

2. SOCIAL POLICY IN THE LATE NINETEEN–EIGHTIES

It is often emphasised that diakonia is an essential expression of the Church's life and being. That is undoubtedly true in principle, but in practice it is perhaps somewhat less than realistic. For in West Germany the *financial enabling* and *legal support* of diaconal work depends only to a small extent on the Church. The laws of the State and the guarantees of performance which they entail underwrite the activities of the Christian social agencies on a scale which the Church cannot match. This being so, all their work depends to a large extent upon on overall developments in social and economic policy in our country. This is a fact, and its consequences for the Church's action should be taken seriously.

It is essential to recognise that the highly developed network of social services is intimately bound up with general economic policy. And it is precisely here that considerable changes have been taking place over the past ten years, changes which inevitably affect the social work of the church. To begin with, whereas in the 60's and 70's production growth rates of 5–6 per cent and more were normal in West Germany, it is now quite plain that a drastic fall has taken place and that growth rates of 2 per cent or thereabouts are likely to be the norm until the end of the century. In consequence, since 1982, the conservative-liberal government has espoused the maxim 'less state and more self-reliance'. The resulting policy has led to a trimming of the welfare budget. Viewed overall, West Germany has not become a poorer country; it is simply that corporate profits are now applied more to modernisation than to welfare.

Then again, 10 years of growing unemployment have placed an increasing burden on the assistance services of the welfare state. Local authorities in particular are feeling these effects, for increasing calls are being made by a growing contingent of long term unemployed on social security benefits, which then become a kind of 'poverty pension'. Apart from that, the physical and mental effects of long lasting unemployment upon individuals are incalculable. It is already apparent that payments for combating the effects of unemployment are rising as a proportion of total welfare expenditure, with a consequent restriction on the financing of aid to handicapped, old and indigent people.

Church agencies alert to developments in social policy should take note that current social and economic policies do not portend developments in the welfare state commensurate with current needs, but rather a radical reorganisation with a significant lowering of costs. What will this mean for the diakonia? One thing is certain: the slimmed-down welfare state of the neo-conservatives will completely change the area in which diakonia operates.

Three forecasts as to the future can even now be formulated:

(a) The diakonia which is part of the Church's structure, and very frequently draws support from local parishes, is particularly well aware of the changes taking place in the composition of the needy groups in society. New forms of poverty, an increase in psychological ailments and other stresses are often detected by the diakonia and supporting Churches before other groups in society become aware of them. In view of the stringency now affecting expenditure on welfare across the board, the Church's agencies will find difficulty in reacting to these new challenges. It does not appear likely that church tax funds will in future account for an increased proportion of the finances of its diakonia, and this means that they will find it difficult in future to meet fresh needs surfacing in our country with new activities.

(b) The social agencies of the Church will be compelled to provide many of their services at a lower cost than hitherto. The criterion of cost is being relentlessly applied to almost every aspect of living, with the result that costs per service are becoming a matter of policy. But there are also bound to be increasing calls on the social services in our society. There will be little financial scope for employing more workers; voluntary help is not inexhaustible either, nor is the self-help principle applicable without limit.

(c) It is likely that, as has happened in the United States, the clientele of the welfare state will become more clearly stratified. A small number of people in need of assistance will be able to maintain the status of paying users and hospitals, old people's home and other institutions; this group will without doubt demand high quality social services, and be prepared to pay for them. By contrast, the overwhelming majority of clients will have to be content with more streamlined services—often enough as recipients of public assistance. Thus the type and extent of the assistance provided will depend more markedly than hitherto on the social status of the person requiring assistance.

3. DIAKONIA AND THE WELFARE STATE CONCEPT

At the present time the diakonia of the Church is doing its work in the context of a welfare state hitherto unsurpassed in terms of social policy. There is undoubtedly a tension between the demands on the welfare state and its reality, and many of the dreams associated with the concept have not yet been translated into practice. Like the diakonia the Church, the welfare state might be better described as a target or objective. All the same, it is incontestable that the diakonia of the Church has received long term resources through association as an element in the welfare state, and an assurance of sustained support, which the churches acting alone could not guarantee. The welfare state constitutes the framework for implementing a task which is a fundamental mark of the essence of the Church and of Christian living, that of service to the community—diakonia. It is a framework not lightly to be disregarded.

Against this background, what about the adage 'He who pays the piper calls the tune'? Should we liken the financing of the Church's social work by the welfare state to a golden chain?

Here briefly are some thoughts on this subject:

(a) The diakonia of the Church is to a large extent dependent financially on what we call for convenience the welfare state. But apart from some friction here and there, the diakonia is free to place the imprint of the Church upon whatever task it is fulfilling. Nevertheless it is debatable whether the quite considerable degree of creative freedom which is allowed places an individual hallmark upon it. The fact that the welfare state is the largest paymaster of the diakonia should not be used as an excuse for failing to operate a hospital or other welfare institution in the spirit of true evangelical commitment to loving service.

(b) It is worth remembering that the welfare state with its financial resources enables the Church to carry on its diakonia. Such work is not a task which might turn out to be dispensable if strict ecclesiastical and theological criteria were applied. Indeed, after proclamation, pastoral care and instruction it is a basic function of the church, one which helps to make the Church truly the Church. Hence with respect to the Church's work in society, the welfare state makes a major contribution towards enabling the Church to be the Church. Viewed in the perspective of church history, this is a somewhat unique situation, scarcely found today in any other developed industrial country. Never has the Church encountered a more favourable environment for her work in society than in the contemporary welfare state.

(c) Many people will ask what is the purpose of constantly taking up collections and making grants from the parishes for the work of the Church's diakonia, when funds are being made available from the church tax, even though the collections and grants do not go far towards paying the expenses of the work. There are two reasons why this practice should be continued—and consciously continued. One is that such gifts encourage the agency receiving them to put the funds to uses that will make plain the Christian content of the service. The other is that through their giving, congregations and individual donors are openly committed to supporting the work of the Church's social agencies and encouraged not to retreat from personal responsibility on the plea that the welfare state will do the job.

4. LEVELS OF OPERATION

We must now make some basic observations about the various operating levels for diaconal work and how they interrelate. In this connection we repeatedly have to deal with the problem of classifying the levels of the church parish, the regional association of churches, and the enterprises. By enterprises I mean the church-based social work complexes which have sometimes been polemically called—mistakenly, in my opinon— 'ecclesiastical Grand-Duchies'; these are enterprises of the diakonia both in the operating and the economic sense.

What then is the problem of classifying the individual operating levels?

When talking about our desire for the diakonia of the Church to be anchored in the parishes, we must be more self-critical in our definition of the parish. From the point of view of church organisation, the parish is of course still the fundamental component of the church, and it is to be hoped that it will so remain. But a parish of that type, parochially organised with regular services and protocol, with instruction and pastoral care and 'a little diakonia' cannot be the primary frame of reference and the sole criterion for the involvement of the Church in society. If it were, then the manifestations of the Church at above local level would be fated to remain simply derivative, secondary and in the last resort superfluous institutions. In an age in which general political developments are giving even national events and institutions a neighbourhood quality, the Church cannot constantly derive its indefeasible claim, the Gospel, to a voice in public affairs and their shaping, simply from neighbourhood structures.

Therefore local parishes should not be at such pains to centre upon themselves diaconal activities which have arisen at regional or national level, or to cultivate a relationship to them. The first requirement is for the parishes to accept the existing division of labour (which after all has to a large extent been organised in the interest of the people who need assistance) whilst recognising and accepting their own responsibility at local level. An imaginative approach locally, below the structures that are regulated and financed by the welfare organisations, can be an important element in the social service activities of the Church. Such imagination is necessary for the sake of the universality of Christian obedience if local parishes do not wish to become simply local distribution networks of a religious ideology. Moreover it is observable that highly imaginative diakonia carried on locally by the Church can—and indeed is bound to—develop many links with the peace movement, inner city work and the ecology movement. The professionalised, entrepreneurially organised social agencies of the Church do not find it easy genuinely to recognise and acknowledge this 'diakonia from below'.

It is of primary importance for Christian social agencies working at interchurch and city level, and for those operating institutions, to be aware that they too are 'parishes' and to let this shine through in their practice. By this I do not mean primarily contact and visiting work in collaboration with local parishes close to or distant from the institution, though that too is important. What I have in mind is rather the indispensable self-demand in all social work for which the Church is responsible—the fact that the parish dimension in inherent from the outset in all its healing, comforting and assistance activities, and this for the sake of the persons needing help, of the helpers, and of increasing fellowship between helpers and helped. This is something that has first to happen inwardly, within a counselling office and a working concept, within a diaconal institution, within a Christian enterprise of diakonia. This of course does not mean that work at regional level should model itself on the lines of a local parish. But all diaconal activities must be approached in such a way that all those involved in the process experience the parish atmosphere.

However, it is not the organisational structures and the interrelations of the various levels of the Church's diakonia that are ultimately decisive. Something more is at stake: The special contribution the Church can make in the field of social work is to seek consistently to discover what happens to people when they are suffering and in need of help, what happens to them in growing up and dying, when they become statistics to government social security offices and are pushed around by overbearing social workers. People's origins and destiny are more or less blotted out by increasingly sophisticated social engineering which takes charge of them from the cradle to the grave, but it may be doubted whether these variants of progress are truly humane. The capacity for growth is atrophied, the power of endurance and the faculty of self-help are being lost. These brief remarks are only intended to indicate that a Church which is active in social work at many levels and in variety of ways must dare to speak out more boldly about human experiences of life and suffering if it is to achieve a credible praxis of Christian diakonia. What is called 'human progress' in the field of social work must be more carefully scrutinised. Only so will Christian diakonia succeed in escaping the ever-present danger of becoming simply custodian of poverty and need in society.

Translated by Alan Braley

Literature consulted

R. Bauer, H. Diessenbacher (Ed.) *Organised love of neighbour* (Opladen 1984).
J. Degen *Diakonie im Widerspruch. Zur Politik der Barmherzigkeit im Sozialstaat* (Munich 1985).
J. Degen *Finanzentwicklung und Finanzstruktur im Bereich der Diakonie* (manuscript 1987).
Deutsche Verein fuer oeffentliche und private Fuersorge (Ed.) *Fachlexikon der sozialen Arbeit* (Frankfurt 1980).
P. Philipp, Diaconia. Über die soziale Dimension kirchlicher Verantwortung (Neukirchen-Vluyn 1984).
Prognos AG, R. Bauer et al *Entwicklung der Freien Wohlfahrtspflege bis zum Jahr 2000* (Basle 1984).
Th. Schober (Ed.) *Gesellschaft als Wirkungsfeld der Diakonie* (Stuttgart 1981).

Gotthard Fuchs

Cultural Diakonia

WHERE THERE is meaningful discussion of diakonia, emergencies play a decisive part—calls for help, objective and subjective, of a structural and a personal nature. At the same time, on the grounds of reason and belief, it is taken for granted that help should and can be given. Jesuanic in its motivation, Christ-centred in its justification and ecclesial in its communication, the service of God (genitive, object and subject!) must be realised. If talk of 'cultural diakonia', as a theological perspective, is to be more than a creatively alienating aperçu, then we must first determine more precisely what we understand by culture (1). Then within the framework of a consideration of general theological principle, we should enquire as to the specific competence of the Church and its task (2). Finally there are at least some topical, cultural emergencies to be discussed under the question of how churches and Christians, themselves affected by these, ought to behave in the spirit of the deacon and prophet from Nazareth (3). Some theses at the end of this outline of the problem (4) are intended to help the work that still has to be done.

1. WHAT IS CULTURE?

The difficulty of obtaining a consistent idea of and for 'culture' (a problem on which every relevant dictionary eloquently informs us) is best tackled by looking at the term historically. It was in fact S. Pufendorf who in 1686 first used the word *cultura* in an absolute sense as the alternative to the natural state of an unformed and instinctive kind, thought to be no longer paradisiac but wretchedly chaotic. Culture henceforth means primarily no longer the caring, forming contact with natural events, but the totality of human life in its individuality and sociality. In this, it was above all the understanding of the historical dimension of social life which, since Herder, became decisive. Culture can therefore be understood in a concrete sense only in historically developing cultures with their peaks and troughs. Seen objectively, culture therefore means interpretations of the world, models of living, language games and paradigms, characteristic of any particular time. Seen subjectively, and in a relationship with the preceding where one is conditioned and illuminated by the other, we are then talking about being cultured: of cultural creativity, of education. By repeating the already 'classic' formulation in *Gaudium et Spes* (No. 53ff.) we can in summary characterise culture as the 'epitome of the historical shaping of a society's means of perception. Included in this are all human material and spiritual achievements which are the premise and basis of man's coping with the world and his social development: the instruments of collective prevention and care in everyday life (medicine, technology), of living together (custom, morality, education, politics, law) and of the interpretation of reality (religion, art, science).'[1]

This all-embracing conception of culture, covering theories of systems and communication, is, it is true, mostly reduced, not only colloquially, to a particular sub-system of society which as such, in distinction to the sub-systems of politics, economy, family etc., is then, in a sense tendentially already isolated, clearly called culture: this is the area of art, literature and science, the area of the 'creators of culture'. In the fixation of this narrowed understanding of culture we find mirrored a highly ambivalent consequence of the differentiation of modern societies. If namely, in the outlines of the classic philosophies of history of the modern era, culture still counted as the univeral communicating form of nature and history, of man and his fellow-men, of individuality and sociality, in the sense of a liberal and just framework, then, because of the economic circumstances, culture henceforth, in reality, wastes away, becoming more and more simply the world of perception of the educated classes, the 'cultured ones' who can more or less afford culture.[2] Culture becomes the luxury of social élites; because they are the ruling class, it is their understanding that becomes the overall yardstick of culture.

The initially Utopian programme, where educational chances were as equal as possible and comprehensive participation in the cultural process was for all, led without doubt to important achievements with regard to the socialisation of knowledge and culture—right up to the present-day education system. But here too the dialectic of enlightenment shows its dark side. Part of this process is the actual devaluation of the prevailing autochthonous and authentic worlds of perception of those who were to be oppressed from now on: those who count as under-developed, as uneducated, as non-cultivated and who become dominated by the levelling-out process of a standardised (non-) culture.

Regional popular cultures, for example, with their richness in particular traditions and well-established modes of behaviour, are discredited, even wiped out—both nationally and internationally and with shocking clarity in the 'Third World'. As a counter to this, it is especially the intellectuals and creators of culture who plead for the positive inheritance of enlightenment and try to work out human alternatives to the cultural imperialism of the educated classes.

Faced with this group of problems and in view of a human race which is in danger of destroying itself and the biosphere, it is justifiable to talk of a global cultural crisis which is, at one and the same time, full of potential and threatening.

2. THE TASK OF THE CHURCH

When Paul VI rightly makes the point in *Evangelii Nuntiandi* (No. 20) that 'the break between Gospel and culture (is) the drama of our time', then this must be seen in concrete terms both with regard to culture as an ensemble of all of society's means of perception and to the sub-system 'culture' in the special sense. At the same time we must at the outset bear in mind that *the* Gospel in concrete terms does not exist in, as it were, chemically isolated 'pure culture'. The writings of the Old and New Testaments are in themselves the document of creative inculturation. Their theological pluralism is at the same time an inter-cultural one (e.g. from the Semitic and Jewish context to the Hellenistic). It is always only in historically conditioned and socio-culturally communicated forms that the Gospel as such comes into language and into the world. At the same time professed forms of living and interpretations of the world are critically absorbed, destroyed and recast in new cultural forms: an inter-cultural process of a kind that is both lengthy and conflict-laden.

At least from the viewpoint of believers alone this process of evangelisatory transformation has diaconic structure, in so far as it tackles the riches and the weaknesses of the cultural contexts it encounters, confronts them with the truth of belief and develops and adds both counter-cultural and even counter-revolutionary alternatives. Because of that, cultural patterns as a whole change in the same way as the social forms of the Gospel itself. This is, in the practice of believers, a genuine historical greatness which, with the goal of redemption and liberation, works its way ever deeper into all the contexts of living. The particular characteristic of this inculturation however is precisely a strange 'exculturative' distance to every historical figure and culture, because it serves the reality of the transcendental God and the coming of his kingdom. Cultural diakonia would therefore have to be characterised as a specific unity of tension embracing both inculturation and exculturation: the service of God completely *in* the world and *for* the world, but not *of* the world. Aggressively added to every culture, the Gospel is determined by and is dependent on no one culture *per se*. The Bible as a whole can in this sense be read as the definitive product and paradigm of cultural diakonia.

It is true that when Paul VI speaks of the tragic break between Gospel and culture, he is not visualising this—theologically necessary—exculturative moment *in* the evangelising process. Rather he is complaining about the gap between the world without God and the Church without the world, of a secular dynamic of self-redemption and the Church existing in a self-created ghetto. *This* kind of exculturation of the Church ought not to be. For whenever church(es) and Christians were spiritually vital, then they were also a cultural factor of rank, without any fear of making contact, without defensive apologetics, with the power to discriminate between minds. (From this point of view of cultural diakonia, the whole history of Christianity and theology could be subjected to a re-reading—right up to cultural protestantism and dialectical theology as Protestant forms of reaction to bourgeois society, and as far as modernism and anti-modernism as their Catholic 'pendant'!)

The question therefore is, if and how far the church(es) and Christians today have or will regain the power of and the competence for cultural diakonia. In this respect there are two things to be learned from the Second Vatican Council and its still controversial reception.

Firstly, the Catholic Church here proved itself capable of learning by creatively absorbing the insights of the modern age which it had up till then rejected (as for example the right to religious freedom). Church is here the 'object' or the receiver of the cultural diakonia of the secular modern age. Where the Church is self-critical to such a degree and accepts help because it reckons on the truth of God as coming from all around, and because it places itself under the Word of God, then the Church itself gains its original competence for cultural diakonia. Otherwise it would—out of anxious worrying about its specific nature—all too easily end up through its own fault in a cultural ghetto.

Secondly, the Council has newly summoned into the general ecclesiastical consciousness the hierarchy of truths and the resulting options, above all for the poor. It is of course above all the aim of the 'counter-culture' revealed by Jesus Christ that finally the victims and the oppressed also are and become subjects of the Beatitudes. Cultural progress, as presented by Christianity, is anti-selective, because it promotes and demands total 'being-as-a-subject' for each and every one. Here is the parameter for cultural diakonia in the name of Jesus.

3. CULTURAL EMERGENCIES

If our considerations so far are now applied in concrete terms to some emergencies and eficiencies in education in particular, then we must remember again the global cultural crisis as a whole and in it the standing of Christianity which is still Western and euro-centrically dominated. What we are looking for are new paradigms of living together for nations and human beings, which permit a just distribution of power, money and knowledge and render oppression as well as the exploitation of man and nature tendentially impossible. Such a 'civilisation of love' and justice would imply a mutually illuminating maximum of sociality and personality (and this with regard to the poor of this world and to future generations) but without furthermore succumbing to anthropocentric narrowing down and reproducing the subsequent destruction of both the world around us and within us.

(a) Expert culture?

One of the dangers of the differentiated society with its tendentially progressive specialisations and segmentations, is that the gap between knowledge of facts and knowledge of the whole becomes ever wider. Being over-informed about details corresponds to being uninformed about the whole, and the cry of help for systematic thinking and behaviour is correspondingly great. As moreover the current systems of knowledge and information have predominantly and unilaterally succumbed and are succumbing to the logic of modern reason characterised by the will to power, so the need for comprehensive knowledge guidelines is blotted out by élitist systems of power knowledge. The desired socialisation and democratisation of this appear to have only limited possibilities under capitalist conditions, however much there are exceptions to the rule.

So the expert culture of the partially informed minorities is paid for by the illiteracy and the non-literacy of the majority: illiteracy means here that the many do not find not only their own language but are being tendentially robbed of their genuine and autochthonous national culture (and national piety); non-literacy means the deficitary and disabling condition of those who are not being helped towards a productive and independent integration of the relative multiplicity of the types of information or towards effecting a creative transformation of them. 'We know more and more and are becoming more and more stupid' (Karl Rahner). This 'cultural lag' is all the more menacing because of the problematic nature of the criteria and controls of the gathering and processing of information.

Cultural diakonia means here re-acquiring for the silent and speechless, according to the promises of the Gospel and the demands of enlightened reason, the ability 'to think *self*, to think oneself in the place of another and to think in unanimity with oneself' (Kant). In this respect it would be important to overcome the gap which has arisen for historical reasons between private educational privilege and the lack of education across the whole of society. The Church must moreover enter into a creative process of literacy with those whose mouths are dead, who have been silenced and robbed of language, in order to find with them and for them the language and identity appropriate to each. At the same time it is important to develop sophisticated strategies against information consumption directed from outside. So the Church has to prove itself as catholic and ecumenical: as the advocate and representative of that lost wholeness which must be regained.

(b) Mass (non-)culture and culture industry

The effect of nationalism led Dietrich Bonhoeffer to write: 'Stupidity is a more dangerous enemy of good than malice. You can protest against evil, you can uncover it, you can in an emergency prevent it by force, evil always carries the seed of self-destruction within itself by leaving behind in people at least the sense of unease. Against stupidity we are defenceless. Neither by protest nor by force can anything be done; giving reasons has no effect; facts contradicting one's own prejudice simply do not need to be believed ...'[3] In abstract terms, we can evoke maturity and 'becoming-as-a-subject' as much as we like, in an appeal both to modern enlightenment as well as, within the Church, to the main conciliar texts—in factual terms, however, the culture industry, guided by special interests, above all by means of the new media, leads often enough to a structural brainwashing and to semi-education in the sense of a mediocre unified culture. In no way should there be any talk here of an abstract chiding of the media. But the danger of a 'gentle dulling of minds' cannot be dismissed. This makes people vulnerable to the ideologies of the left and right; it makes them insensitive, indeed blind to the urgent challenges of the present.

Cultural diakonia must here take the form of the courage to think laterally, to criticise contexts which blind and dazzle, 'opening wounds in the fields of habit' (Nelly Sachs) and developing alternatives to alternatives which no longer dull the mind but release subjectivity and shared subjectivity, that is to say, solidarity. The struggle of 'simple', 'uneducated' people to gain entry to the culture of the educated classes in the nineteenth and twentieth century in

Europe, in the late twentieth century in the 'Third World', offers ample 'illustrative material' for the efforts that are needed. cultural diakonia then has the further meaning of creatively questioning prevailing plausibilities and working uncomfortable or forgotten themes into the social discourse. In a short-lived instant culture it is for example a particular service to remember 'dangerously' in its topicality the richness of experience of past times.

(c) Counter-culture

The particular profile we have of intellectuals, artists and 'creators of culture' is the result of their exhausting efforts, in the sense of secularised prophecy, to achieve a false permanence, and of their creating the beginnings of counter-cultures—*in* the existing framework of living and for its further development. The attitude of criticism has become a decisive factor here—criticism not in the sense of carping but in the manner of resolute negation. Everything can and must—in a highly self-critical way—be quoted before the judgement seat of theoretical and practical reason. Only by undergoing such a deliberate calling into question can we, just possibly, arrive at a second naiveté. Without this critical pathos the cultural life of (post-)modernism and (post-) modernism itself cannot be understood.

The biases and dangers connected with this are, without doubt, in need of the corrective offered by cultural diakonia. This is all the more valid as the message and life's work of Jesus Christ Himself can be described as counter-cultural initiatives. But nowhere does the break between gospel and culture—more accurately between church(es) and modernism—become so painful as here (in which connection, the widely differing forms of this break, as they appear among the various denominations, must remain unconsidered here). In factual terms, intellectuals to a large extent experience the Roman Catholic Church in the German Federal Republic as exculturated. The Church is not a creative factor in the fields of art and literature. On the other hand, it is a valid point that the richness of experience of the ecclesiastical internal culture and its history has to a large extent been lost in the total social consciousness.

Cultural diaconate then means in the first instance being aware of and not suppressing the extent and depth of the break. At the present time one probably should talk, in actual fact, of an exculturation of the Catholic Church in this area. It therefore needs an internal ecclesiastical renewal to achieve that link with the intellectual and cultural level of modernism which the Council suggested and inaugurated. Such a cultural diakonia of the Church *ad intra*, into the area of its own life and belief, appears imperative in order to regain the necessary competence in diakonia *ad extra*, into society as a whole. It is significant for example that the newly emerging religious question—and this applies also to 'educated people amongst those who hold it in contempt'—to a large extent overlooks ecclesiastical Christianity in its search for answers. Cultural diakonia has to emphasise the 'surplus value' of Christian tradition (and mysticism) in a creative and attractive way—in order all the more to insist also, in a productive lack of simultaneity, on the discrimination of minds.

(d) Inter-cultural dialogue

The present situation seems amongst other things to be characterised by the fact that in West European societies (and churches) more and more people have the feeling that the whole prevailing cultural system is having a destructive effect and requires fundamental change. Not a few are opting out and seeking radical alternatives. At the same time, beyond the respective cultural horizon, interest is growing in other contexts of tradition and communities of interpretation. Side by side with the danger of syncretism, there is here a special opportunity. In fact, to the advantage of a polycentric world culture and Church community, there is the need for the necessary mixture of humility and self-awareness, of faithfulness to one's own cultural tradition as well as the readiness to let outmoded forms of culture die and subsume them into a larger, more varied cultural totality of events. World Church can in this sense contribute specifically to the formation of a spirituality and sophistication on a world scale, in which regional particular cultures and specific characteristic traditions of groups, regions, nations etc., will no longer be suppressed or indeed obliterated, but will come into their own. This means also developing a dialogue ethic of mutual respect, a culture of inter-religious and inter-cultural dialogue.

'From that point ways open up to a deeper accommodation in the totality of Christian life. If one proceeds in such a way, every appearance of syncretism and false particularism is excluded; the Christian life is accommodated to the spirit and individuality of every culture; the particular traditions, together with the gifts of the different families of nations illuminated by the Gospel, are received into the Catholic unity' (Second Vatican Council: *Ad gentes* 22).

At the same time it will become ever clearer how very much the social and doctrinal form of Christianity up to now bears a Western imprint and needs to return to the melting-pot in order to be an effective ferment of the desired world culture. Cultural diakonia therefore encompassea a specifically European-North Atlantic selflessness in favour of this universal cultural process. From that, particular cultures will, on the other hand, acquire a new dignity and quality.

4. THESES

Some important results of this outline of the problem can be summarised in the form of theses:

(a)　Culture can—in the sense of the last Council—be understood as the universal medium of the Gospel and its communication. The Gospel of the Old and New Testaments for its part presupposes and releases culture(s) as a reality of creation. It does this by asserting itself and being confirmed as a final orientation transcending all culture(s). Cultural diakonia is then identical with evangelisation itself from the point of view of the equally critical and creative acceptance of each culture. It enters a new context of understanding, action and interpretation. Its demons are driven out and it is set free to a state of freedom, justice and love. The Gospel for its part is experienced in concrete terms only in this socio-cultural process and partially develops cultural areas of its own.

(b)　Culture can—in the sense of the last Council—be understood as a particular area of society for the total interpretation of reality and for the establishing as well as the preserving of a public ethos. Cultural diakonia then means entering, on the part of Christian belief, into a mutually critical and creative cultural exchange (for example with art, literature etc.). This includes the courage to reveal emergencies and to work to overcome them wherever possible in a vicarious offensive. This inter-cultural service is mutual in so far as Church is, in itself, a historically determined area of culture which, for its part, is in need of constant reform (particularly at a time when it threatens to adopt a ghetto mentality).

(c)　Subjects of cultural diakonia are church(es) and Christians. Recipients of its service are 'the world', society, the whole framework of culture and its particular areas. This definition is theologically apt, in so far as church(es) and Christians are of the belief that with the Gospel they bear witness to a truth which is unique and without alternatives. The result of that is their sense of self and mission in terms of diakonia. It would however be a fatally wrong conclusion if one were to consider church(es) and Christians for their part as not standing in need of cultural diakonia. Often they have in fact enough cultural deficiencies which impair their role in contemporary society and their credibility. Only when one understands God himself in his service to the world as a subject of cultural diakonia as well, will one do theological justice to the facts.

Translated by Gordon Wood

Notes

1. Hans-Joachim Höhn *Kirche und kommunikatives Handeln. Studien zur Theologie und Praxis der Kirche in der Auseinandersetzung mit den Sozialtheorien Niklas Luhmanns und Jürgen Habermas* (Frankfurt 1985) 172 (Lit.); cf., Linus Hauser *Theologie und Kiltur. Transzendentale theologische Reflexionen zu ihrer Interdependenz* (Altenberg 1983).

2. See Helmut Peukert *Über die Zukunft der Bildung* (Frankfurter Hefte Extra 6 1984) 129–137.

3. Dietrich Bonhoeffer *Widerstand und Ergebung* (Munich 1977) 16f.

Prospect

Ulrich Bach

'But if you say so!' A Plea for a Church of the Diakonia

HOW SHOULD I argue for something that has never existed? A plea for a Cloud-cuckoo-land would be no use to anyone. On the contrary, it might lead to resignation among those anxious to encourage in a particular parish some evidence of what we might term a 'diaconal atmosphere'. They might be discouraged. If *that*'s a 'Church of the diakonia', then we're better off without it, I should say. The tragicomedy would be complete. The conception behind my plea for a diaconal Church might rule out some courageous measures leading to one. In other words, my very argument for a Church of the diakonia would nip the growing plant in the bud. But, surely then, if a plea for a diaconal Church is not to bring about the opposite of what is intended, we must take all acutal manifestations of an approach to the diaconal Church more seriously than that 'Church of the diakonia itself'.

What exactly are we talking about when we use such terms? It is simpler to say what we are *not* talking about. We are not concerned with a Church that would be a 'Church of the diakonia' as a result of all-out effort and appropriate organisation. Our efforts, to be sure, could lead us to extend and broaden the so-called 'diakonia of the Church'. It might be, let us say, any parish with at least an old people's home, or with a school for special needs, or with an addicts' advice centre. No one could ever object to that. But the Church of the diakonia means something else: not, indeed, a Church which 'has' a well-organised diakonia (for then the diakonia would be a sector of the Church), but a Church in which diakonia is the basic structural element. A church, therefore, which as a matter of principle 'is' diaconal in all its discourse, activity and organisation. (Then diakonia is an essential—or indeed, the essential—dimension of the Church). But we *have* achieved something. For example, we use the same text of the Lord's Prayer in all German-speaking parishes. There *is* something we *could* achieve. We could become a 'singing Church', for instance by appointing a cantor to each parish, and by ensuring that there is no religious service or Sunday school without singing. But there is something else that we shall not bring about before Judgement Day ... I mean, we shall not become a Church of saints in which there is no more sin and no trace of unbelief or doubt. There is just as small a chance that we shall become a Church of diakonia in which there is no longer any evidence of anything un-diaconal.

1. ESSENTIALS OF A DIACONAL CHURCH

Again, what do we mean when we talk of the Church of the diakonia, or of the diaconal Church? I cannot offer a definition here, but I can list a few essential components.

(*a*) Church of the least among us

A church of the diakonia would be a 'Church of the least among us'. It is so very important to attend to the needy. It is fundamentally important to accept that Jesus recommended his disciples to play the part of the least. He called them 'the least of these my brethren' (Matt. 25:31ff). He asked them to surrender all forms of rule (of the kind usual in the world). Instead a Christian ought to be 'servant of all' (Mark 10:4ff).[1] The washing of feet was not to be something unique, but an 'example' (John 13:15). The way in which Jesus behaved towards his disciples became the way in which we should behave towards one another.

(*b*) Church of the first commandment

The Church of the diakonia would be a Church of the first commandment. We are to fear and to love God before all else, and to place our trust in him (Luther in his *Small Catechism*). Henceforth we must acknowledge our ungodly associates. Often we are not 'servants' of our fellow humans, but slaves of certain norms and ideals: 'The main thing is good health'. All of us have said and thought that or something like it, even if we have not always been so consistent as the young man who told me more than thirty years ago (I was a student and had been in a wheelchair for about a year and a half): 'In your place I would have made an end of things long ago.' Then there are other 'main things' of the first and second order (achievement, an intact family, education, property, not having a police record) which prevent us from loving God 'before all else'. 'My grace is sufficient for you' is what Paul heard (2 Cor. 12:9). Often it *doesn't* seem sufficient. We want grace *and* success, grace *and* respect from others, grace *and* non-handicapped children. We even want God's grace to consist of giving us success, respect and so on. (This kind of thinking endangers the unity of the Church, for then everyone who is less successful, or whose child is handicapped, becomes someone who clearly is less endowed with divine grace. 'I' want to be the Lord, and ultimtely God should see to that. 'A man cannot by nature desire that God should be God; rather *he* wishes that *he* were God and God were not God! (Luther, 1517: *Disputation against Scholastic Theology*, thesis 17). *There* is the essential reason why—even with theological phraseology—we separate people into those of higher and lower quality. Theological thought on the 'Church of the diakonia' therefore has to conceive of itself as liberation theology pure and simple. Those alternatives which we all find are always important— healthy/sick, imprisoned/free, west/east, handicapped/non-handicapped, energetic late forties/dotty old man (and so forth)—have to be unmasked as the enslaving idols they are. Depending on which side we are on, these alternatives can even prove expensive. We often fail to notice how they are ruining us; the connection with the God of the first commandment (cf. Exod. 20:1: 'I who led you out of bondage'), who bestows himself on us as God for us, and who summons us into his everlasting covenant, is to be proclaimed in contradistinction as the sole way to freedom, to the 'freedom of the children of God'.

(c) Church as the Body of Christ

The Church of the diakonia would be a Church which saw itself as the Body of Christ. We are very different members and organs, but that does not signify any special claims. Everyone is important in his or her place—as important as others in their places. That has two implications: we are not here for our on sakes, but for the whole (here something is asked by others). On the other hand, we are not our own yardstick, we need others (we don't very much like to hear that, for 'self-sufficiency' is the name of another idol that grips us in its claws). Paul maintains that the statement 'I have no need of you' (1 cor. 12:21) is a godless statement which is quite inappropriate to the Body of Christ'.

It seems that we Christians are subject to an apparently pious but actually quite unbiblical and élitist delusion which persuades us that we should always be 'in service', and any 'Can you help me out with this?' seems to contradict Jesus's commission to us. Why do we resist this—Everyone is part of the

Body, and must strive to do everything on his or her own—Is that how we are constituted?

(d) Church in which we get along together

The Church of the diakonia would be a Church in which the differences between us are not whitewashed but are deprived of any divisive function. 'There is neither Jew nor Greek, there is neither bond nor free, there is neither male nor female; for you are all *one* in Christ Jesus' (Gal. 3:28). Of course there are 'Jews and Greeks' among us, yet we get along together. Of course there are men and women among us—yet we get along together. Of course, there are handicapped and non-handicapped people among us, yet we get along together.[2] But we often find it important *not* to get along with 'those particular people'. In our Volmarstein vocational centre, a very slightly handicapped youth described how they accompanied a group of handicapped people to the shops in the neighbouring town of Hagen. 'The people there just couldn't stop staring at us in a funny way' ... And there were complaints about a society which had such strong objections 'to people like us'. I said: 'If you walk through Hagen on your own, does anyone look at you?'—'No.'—'And yet you're annoyed now because people stare at others in wheelchairs?'—'Yes, of course'.—'Well, *couldn't* it be that *you* were annoyed to be one of a group which people stared at intolerantly?'—'Well, yes. Yes, that's true. Yes, of course—that was it'. He didn't want to be taken for one of the others. That was part of his self-image: 'Yes, I'm handicapped, but it's hardly noticeable, people don't stare at me—I'm not one of *those*.'—And then, for once, he was *one of those'*. Anyone, surely, would find that disturbing.

I have not defined the 'Church of the diakonia' as it ought to be. Yet the sparse hints I have offered are enough to support the view that the Church of the diakonia is something that we shall never be able to 'attain to' or 'make'. Why not? The answer seems almost trivial. We are human. As long as we humans are in the world, we shall never be free of the non-sacred, of sin and doubt, nor of the non-diaconal: the conceit of our self-elevating selves. Perhaps not only to know this (as information) but to have learned it (through experience) is a first major stop on the road to our liberation.

(e) Church for the handicapped

When I became aware of the foregoing partly after getting to know the mentally handicapped and their parents and helpers. How can one avoid directing people in this area? A person accompanying a handicapped individual must constantly decide important things, and make decisions on the other's behalf. One may be able to say (or indicate) that he or she has toothache, but a lecture on the 'free choice' of a doctor is too much to expect. Someone else has to decide which dentist to consult. All day long many decisions have to be made on the same basis. However conscious the principle may be that we have to distinguish 'potestas' (the power which is used to maintain and promote the life of others) from 'potentia' (the power which is exerted to one's own advantage and at others' expense), who could define the boundaries in practice (in *this* praxis) exactly? Anyone who says that it is possible to live with severely mentally handicapped people and at the same time to avoid domination—which is forbidden in principle anyway—just has no conception of what a large and important sector of the 'basis' of our society is actually like.[3]

(*f*) Church for the suffering

I learnt a second point from Peter. When Jesus speaks of his suffering (Matt. 16:21), Peter objects that it cannot be the will of God. I recognised myself in this Peter. I too want God to be different (I rebel against the first commandment). I want a God who helps us to escape suffering, who saves himself from the Cross and averts our own crosses. I am glad that in his rebuttal of Peter's objection, Jesus confirms Peter's thinking and reaction as 'human'. You are thinking not along divine but human lines. Therefore Jesus thinks: You see this in a typically human way, Peter, when you cannot reconcile 'God' and the 'the Cross'. For *my own part* (since I rediscovered myself in Peter): As long as you are a human being, things cannot change. You don't want suffering and so you want God to specialise in doing things to prevent suffering.

(*g*) Church of the dying

I also learnt this third point from Jesus, when I was 'with him' as he prayed in Gethsemane (Matt. 26:39) ... The Son of God said: 'I do not want to go on the Cross.' Jesus didn't say: 'I want to if you really want it.' And he certainly didn't say (that would be something like Peter's line in Matt. 16): 'Please adapt your will to my notions of 'just' and 'good'. But Jesus also didn't say (for that would be the Stoic attitude—I want everything that happens): 'Adapt my will to your will. Please make me want what you find 'good'? No. Jesus clearly leaves it as an antithesis of 'I want' and 'You want'. Jesus is so very human that he cannot want the cross. He is so honest as to admit that openly. He is obedient (of., Phil. 2:8), so obedient that he is ready to follow the path which he abhors. 'Let your will prevail over mine. Not as I want, but as you want.' I find this prayer of Jesus's important in my thinking about the Church of the diakonia. If a diaconal Church is the 'Church of the first commandment', and therefore a Church which knows nothing more important than God and the will of God and his way with us; and if on the other hand even Jesus did not want what God wanted, then it seems clear to me that the diaconal Church is not something quantitative which we all fundamentally want. Rather, the Church of the diakonia has to do with letting oneself be led along a certain path against one's will—with penitence—while acknowledging God's justice even when it is contrary to our own desires; therefore while accepting that God vanquishes (not my sin, death the devil, but) us; with dying—not with dying into nothing, but with the seed that only brings forth fruit when it dies (John. 12:24)—thus, with dying towards hope. It has to do with doing without: giving up being the high-point of one's own life; doing without being able to pre-programme the results of one's own actions and pain (the dying seed cannot wish and cannot plan the 'fruit', yet it appears). It has to do with surrendering oneself wholly to God (Jesus could only die on Golgotha. He could not determine Easter. Easter was no longer his concern. *God made* Easter Jesus' concern.) Thus we do not attain to the diaconal Church by listening only to our inner voices, which allow what slumbers within us to unfold. If what lies inherent in us emerges, then at best the result would be an impressive major social conglomerate (with several major and minor shareholders), but the diaconal Church is something other than that.

(*h*) Church where we only go so far

The fourth point I learnt from a teacher of the handicapped. She told me about the school class where she taught seriously and multiply handicapped young people. It was impossible to teach them counting and writing but, for example, conscious reactions to various stimuli (round/angular, smooth/rough, soft/hard objects), body movements to musical rhythms and so on. She said that there was much more laughter in her classroom than in a normal school class. She also said that she could only do this work because she had colleagues to whom she could say: 'I only got so far with Gerda again today, that I wondered whether it wouldn't really be better for her and for all of us if she wasn't there any longer'. She can say that without anyone replying; 'And you think you are a Christian and a teacher of the handicapped!' As long as we remain human beings, certain encounters must prompt thoughts of euthanasia (even in us Christians). Anyone who doesn't know that has only got to know a very limited group of his or her fellow humans, or else is not yet properly aware of himself or herself.

Therefore we have to be clear that the 'Church of the diakonia' is not a goal towards which we are travelling so that one day we can say: 'Here we are at last!' We never reach *that* destination. What does this mean? Is the diaconal Church a phantasm like 'Cloud-cuckoo-land' and a 'perfect world'? It is a good idea to take a kind of mental break when handling such ideas, and indeed we must admit that this means we are fleeing from our reality. Surely then we should stop talking about it ...

2. BUT IF YOU SAY SO

At the beginning I said that the Church of the diakonia had never existed. That is still the case. Yet it is not a phantasm. For there was, if not a diaconal Church, a diaconal peson. Without the human being Jesus of Nazareth, the diaconal Church would indeed remain a Cloud-cuckoo-land. If this Jesus had not been raised through God as a the Lord over all, then our efforts in this respect would be the phantasies of a Don Quixote.

Jesus was the diaconal human being. He accorded God the honour. He was the only one to keep to the first commandment, and to give God total precedence over self. He, the highest of all, the universal creator (without him was nothing made that was made, John. 1:3), was the least of all. He lay in a manger (Luke 2). He was poorer than foxes and birds (Mark 10:45f). He did not set himself apart but became quite like unto us ('and was made in the likeness of men', Phil. 2:7). He had such close contact with the lower depths of his own society that he was known as the 'friend of ... sinners' (Matt. 11:19). In the hour of his death he could indeed be taken for an other. Now three criminals were hanging on their crosses. He entered the society of the needy. He helped where he could and was not too proud to ask for help too.[4] Therefore Christians called him the 'head of the body' (Col. 1:18). This Jesus, this diaconal peson, summons us to follow him. We cannot achieve what he achieved, but we should *follow his way*. If we do follow him how many kilometres or millimetres we have 'done' and what route we are on are important.

The remainder ought not really to be of any importance at all. I mean our bulging, stumbling, failures. It would be important for us and quite unsettling if the human being Jesus had *not* been elevated by God as the Lord over all things. His presence on this road we take is accordingly more serious than our failures along it. 'See, I am with you all days ...' (Matt. 28:20). We 'cannot' follow this road in the same way that Peter (Luke 5) 'could not' catch fish. 'But if you say so!' (Luke 5:5) Peter does go ahead. That is what it is about: our being ready to act at his word when he calls us to follow him, to begin to follow the diaconal person Jesus, conscious of his forgiveness, and trusting that the

God who created the world from nothing and who makes the dead live, also has the power to make even our insignificant efforts precious elements in his construction.

'But if you say so'—for a Church setting out towards a Church 'of the diakonia' this must be its only slogan, constant prayer, universally rehearsed fundamental attitude, and similarly the principle of all its thought, discourse and activity: 'But if you say so'.

As far as our theology and proclamation are concerned, that means that they must speak of all people uniformly and without restriction. If we (for example) call humankind God's good creation, then we are necessarily forbidden to say in respect of a severely handicapped individual that he or she is 'naturally', 'also', 'still', 'somehow' a creature of God. That *every* human being is that good creature willed and made by God is something that 'one can' say just as little as Peter 'could' catch fish—'But if you say so!' Some years ago I noted what a participant at a conference said: 'There are steps not only in edifices but in edification'. Whta we need is a 'ground floor' theology and proclamation.[5] That doesn't mean a special theology or special proclamation for the disadvantaged, but a biblical theology, and that always means a theology for the ordinary and insignificant and one accessible to all.

What is the basis of our praxis, the spirit of our life-style, the 'word' which imbues our communal striving? Surely we are too ready to adapt to what is thought and said and done round about us? 'But if you say so!' henceforth we have to venture a new praxis in our parishes, a praxis in which—sometimes at least—the last are first. It has to be one in which we have the 'munificence' to be small and to take the interests of a child as seriously as church on Sunday. It must be one in which 'a career downwards'[6] is neither a joke nor a sacred formula but lived reality (the article in question is to some extent a *report* on the 'Münster Non-resident Aid Centre'). It has to be a praxis which conceives of itself as a 'counterworld to belief in progress, the claim to happiness, the achievement ideology, and compulsive consumption'.[7] We 'cannot' do any of that—'But if you say so!'

Then we make ourselves ridiculous. That is the sort of thing 'one' does not do. In the end there must be 'certain limits' for we can't lose face. Here, it seems, our churches are up against a major decision. Are we afraid of losing face? As long as we have this fear we are just not moving towards a diaconal Church. Or are we aware that the 'face' of the Church can only be composed in God; that for that reason by definition it cannot go wrong? Are we then to be drawn (by his 'Word') into the 'glorious liberty of the children of God' (Rom. 8:21)?

3. TOWARDS THE FORM OF DIAKONIA

It is neither promised nor laid down that we should attain the finished form of a diaconal Church. But, following Jesus' summons towards the Church of the diakonia—awkwardly and falteringly—is a process called 'But if you say so' in which we are engaged ever anew.

Translated by J. G. Cumming

Notes

1. U. Bach *Dem Traum enstagen, mehr als ein Mensch zu sein* (1986) pp. 73ff.
2. On the 'Yes but ... ' attitude see U. Bach, *Boden unter den Füssen hat keiner* (1980) pp 25ff, 137f.
3. I cite in this regard two directors of major institutions for mentally handicapped people: Johannes Klevinghaus; in *Evang. Theol-* (1950) p. 238: 'The barrier between being entrusted and being delivered up is paper-thin/ Diakonia and power lie alongside one another. Happy he who finds his brother, but let him beware who falls into the hands of men!'—See also Joachim Klieme In *Zur Orientierung* (1985), nos 3/4, p. 240: 'After all every form of care, education and formation of the handicapped is indeed the turning of one human being to another, but also presumption between human beings'.
4. See U. Bach *Kraft in leeren Händen* (1983) pp. 14–16, 57 ff, 119; and so on.
5. See U. Bach *Dem Traum entsagen* ...op. cit., pp. 113ff; also: O. Fuchs, in: *Beitrage zur korper-behinderten Fürsorge* (No. 40), pp. 6ff passim.
6. The title which Ursula Adams gave to an article in 1979. In *Geist und leben* pp 201ff.

Contributors

CARLOS ABESAMIS SJ studied theology in the state university in Innsbruck, 1960–64, and Scripture at the Pontifical Biblical Institute in Rome, 1966–68. He acts as theological consultant for the National Secretariat for Social Action, Justice and Peace of the Catholic Bishops Conference. He co-founded the Socio-Pastoral Institute, was a founding member of the Ecumenical Association of Third World Theologians, and holds seminars and workshops on the general topic of Re-Reading the Bible in the Third World. His publications include *Where are We Going: Heaven or New World?* (1983/86); *Exploring the Core of Biblical Faith* (1986); *The Mission of Jesus and Good News to the Poor* (1987).

ADEBAYO ADEDEJI is a Nigerian Anglican based in Addis Ababa (Ethiopia). He is an UN Under-secretary-general, and Executive Secretary of the Economic Commission for Africa.

ULRICH BACH was born in 1931. He has an honorary doctorate of the Protestant theological faculty of Bochum University. In 1951 he began a theology course and after his third term he became a polio victim. From 1955 to 1958 he completed his studies (in a wheelchair). After a short time working in Wittekindshof (Institute for the Mentally Handicapped) and Dortmund, since 1962 he has been a minister at the Volmarstein (Ruhr) Orthopaedic Institution, and Lecturer in New Testament and in Dogmatic Theology at the Martineum Diaconate (Volkmarstein, then Witten/Ruhr). He is the author of various books, in particular on diakonia and prayer.

GREGORY BAUM was born in Berlin in 1923 and has been resident in Canada since 1940. He was a student at McMaster University in Hamilton, Canada, in the University of Fribourg, Switzerland, and at Ohio State University as well as at the New School for Social Research in New York. He is now Professor of Theology and Sociology at St Michael's College, University of Toronto. He is editor of the journal *The Ecumenist*. Publications include *Man Becoming* (1970); *New Horizon* (1972); *Religion and Alienation* (1975); *The Social Imperative* (1978); *Catholics and Canadian Socialism* (1980); *The Priority of Labor* (1982); *Ethics and Economics* (1984).

FREI BETTO is a Dominican brother, living in São Paulo, where he is an adviser on pastoral practice and Christian base communities. He studied journalism, philosophy and theology, and was twice arrested under the military regime in Brazil, spending four years in prison. He has also worked with base communities in Nicaragua and since 1981 has worked with the Cuban Government on matters concerning Church and religion in Latin America. He has visited the Soviet Union as guest of the Orthodox Church, and Poland at the invitation of government and Church. His published books include a novel and a volume of short stories, as well as *L'Eglise des prisons* (1972), *Brasilienische Passion* (1973), *Against Principalities and Powers* (1977), *Diario di Puebla* (1979), *Les Frères de Tito* (1984) and *Fidel y la Religión* (1985).

NORBERT BROX was born on 23 June 1935 in Paderborn. He is a Catholic. He holds a doctorate in theology, qualified as a university lecturer in patrology and ecumenical studies, and is at present Professor in Early Church History and Patrology at the University of Regensburg. Recent publications include *Falsche Verfasserangaben* (1975); *Salvian von Marseille, Des Timotheus vier Bücher an die Kirche* (1983); *Der erste Petrusbrief* (1986); *Kirchengeschichte des Altertums* (1986).

ELISABETH SCHÜSSLER FIORENZA, is Krister Stendahl Professor at Harvard Divinity School Massachusetts. She is past president of the Society of Biblical Literature and founding co-editor of the *Journal of Feminist Studies in Religion* and committed to women-church. Recent publications include *In Memory of Her: A Feminist theological Reconstruction of Early Christian Origins*; *The Book of Revelation: Judgement and Justice*; and *Bread not Stone: The Challenge of Feminist Biblical Interpretation*.

GOTTHARD FUCHS, born 1938 in Halle/Saale, studied philosophy and Catholic theology and was ordained priest in 1963. He has been active for many years in spiritual welfare and counselling as well as a member of the theological faculties in Münster and Bamberg. Since 1983 he has been director of the Catholic Academy Rabanus Maurus of the dioceses of Fulda, Limburg and Mainz. Publications include *Belief as Resistance* (1986); in collaboration with H. H. Henrix: *Saving Time. The Messianic Thought of Franz Rosenzweig* (1987); he has also written frequent essays on theological and spiritual questions.

OTTMAR FUCHS was born in 1945. After studying philosophy and theology in Bamberg and Würzburg, he was engaged in pastoral work in

Nuremberg before becoming student chaplain in Bamberg. Since 1982 he has been professor for pastoral theology and kerygmatics in the Catholic theological faculty of Bamberg University.

NORBERT METTE was born in 1946 in West Germany, studied theology and social science and is now Professor of practical theology at the Paderborn university joint college. He is a member of the governing committee of CONCILIUM. He has published widely on pastoral theology and religious education. Recent publications include *Voraussetzung christlicher Elementarerziehung* (1983); *Kirche auf dem Weg ins Jahr 2000* (with M. Blasberg-Kuhnke 1986); *Gemeindepraxis in Grundbegriffen* (with Chr. Baeumler 1987).

HERMANN STEINKAMP was born in 1938 and studied theology, philosophy and sociology at Münster, Munich, Bonn and Würzburg. He gained his D.Phil. in 1966 and his D. Theol. under Wilhelm Dreier in Würzburg in 1972. From 1968 to 1975 he lectured at the Akademie für Jugendfragen. From 1969 to 1973 he was research assistant at the Institut für christliche Sozialwissenschaft at the University of Würzburg, and since 1974 he has been Professor of Pastoral Sociology and the educational theory of religion (*Religionspädagogik*) at Münster. Publications include *Gruppendynamik und Demokratisierung* (1972); *Jugendarbeit als soziales Lernen* (1977, [2]1979); *Sozialwissenschaft und praktische Theologie* (1983); and *Diakonie—Kennzeichen der Gemeinde* (1985).

PATRICK KALILOMBE, former bishop of Lilongwe in Malawi, is presently lecturer in Third World Theologies and Primal World Views at the Selly Oak Colleges, Birmingham. Recently he took up the directorship of the centre for Black and White Christian Partnership, a part of the Selly Oak federation. This Centre strives to promote understanding and cooperation between the mainline churches in Britain (White-led churches) and the numerous Black-led independent churches of Caribbean and West African origins, in view of joint mission in multi-cultural Britain.

CONCILIUM

1. (Vol. 1 No. 1) **Dogma.** Ed. Edward Schillebeeckx. 86pp.
2. (Vol. 2 No. 1) **Liturgy.** Ed. Johannes Wagner. 100pp.
3. (Vol. 3 No. 1) **Pastoral.** Ed. Karl Rahner. 104pp.
4. (Vol. 4 No. 1) **Ecumenism.** Hans Küng. 108pp.
5. (Vol. 5 No. 1) **Moral Theology.** Ed. Franz Bockle. 98pp.
6. (Vol. 6 No. 1) **Church and World.** Ed. Johannes Baptist Metz. 92pp.
7. (Vol. 7 No. 1) **Church History.** Roger Aubert. 92pp.
8. (Vol. 8 No. 1) **Canon Law.** Ed. Teodoro Jimenez Urresti and Neophytos Edelby. 96pp.
9. (Vol. 9 No. 1) **Spirituality.** Ed. Christian Duquoc. 88pp.
10. (Vol. 10 No. 1) **Scripture.** Ed. Pierre Benoit and Roland Murphy. 92pp.
11. (Vol. 1 No. 2) **Dogma.** Ed. Edward Shillebeeckx. 88pp.
12. (Vol. 2 No. 2) **Liturgy.** Ed. Johannes Wagner. 88pp.
13. (Vol. 3 No. 2) **Pastoral.** Ed. Karl Rahner. 84pp.
14. (Vol. 4 No. 2) **Ecumenism.** Ed. Hans Küng. 96pp.
15. (Vol. 5 No. 2) **Moral Theology.** Ed. Franz Bockle. 88pp.
16. (Vol. 6 No. 2) **Church and World.** Ed. Johannes Baptist Metz. 84pp.
17. (Vol. 7 No. 2) **Church History.** Ed. Roger Aubert. 96pp.
18. (Vol. 8 No. 2) **Religious Freedom.** Ed. Neophytos Edelby and Teodoro Jimenez Urresti. 96pp.
19. (Vol. 9 No. 2) **Religionless Christianity?** Ed. Christian Duquoc. 96pp.
20. (Vol. 10 No. 2) **The Bible and Tradition.** Ed. Pierre Benoit and Roland E. Murphy. 96pp.
21. (Vol. 1 No. 3) **Revelation and Dogma.** Ed. Edward Schillebeeckx. 88pp.
22. (Vol. 2 No. 3) **Adult Baptism and Initiation.** Ed. Johannes Wagner. 96pp.
23. (Vol. 3 No. 3) **Atheism and Indifference.** Ed. Karl Rahner. 92pp.
24. (Vol. 4 No. 3) **The Debate on the Sacraments.** Ed. Hans Küng. 92pp.
25. (Vol. 5 No. 3) **Morality, Progress and History.** Ed. Franz Bockle. 84pp.
26. (Vol. 6 No. 3) **Evolution.** Ed. Johannes Baptist Metz. 88pp.
27. (Vol. 7 No. 3) **Church History.** Ed. Roger Aubert. 92pp.
28. (Vol. 8 No. 3) **Canon Law— Theology and Renewal.** Ed. Neophytos Edelby and Teodoro Jimenez Urresti. 92pp.
29. (Vol. 9 No. 3) **Spirituality and Politics.** Ed. Christian Duquoc. 84pp.
30. (Vol. 10 No. 3) **The Value of the Old Testament.** Ed. Pierre Benoit and Roland Murphy. 92pp.
31. (Vol. 1 No. 4) **Man, World and Sacrament.** Ed. Edward Schillebeeckx. 84pp.
32. (Vol. 2 No. 4) **Death and Burial: Theology and Liturgy.** Ed. Johannes Wagner. 88pp.

33. (Vol. 3 No. 4) **Preaching the Word of God.** Ed. Karl Rahner. 96pp.
34. (Vol. 4 No. 4) **Apostolic by Succession?** Ed. Hans Küng. 96pp.
35. (Vol. 5 No. 4) **The Church and Social Morality.** Ed. Franz Bockle. 92pp.
36. (Vol. 6 No. 4) **Faith and the World of Politics.** Ed. Johannes Baptist Metz. 96pp.
37. (Vol. 7 No. 4) **Prophecy.** Ed. Roger Aubert. 80pp.
38. (Vol. 8 No. 4) **Order and the Sacraments.** Ed. Neophytos Edelby and Teodoro Jimenez Urresti. 96pp.
39. (Vol. 9 No. 4) **Christian Life and Eschatology.** Ed. Christian Duquoc. 94pp.
40. (Vol. 10 No. 4) **The Eucharist: Celebrating the Presence of the Lord.** Ed. Pierre Benoit and Roland Murphy. 88pp.
41. (Vol. 1 No. 5) **Dogma.** Ed. Edward Schillebeeckx. 84pp.
42. (Vol. 2 No. 5) **The Future of the Liturgy.** Ed. Johannes Wagner. 92pp.
43. (Vol. 3 No. 5) **The Ministry and Life of Priests Today.** Ed. Karl Rahner. 104pp.
44. (Vol. 4 No. 5) **Courage Needed.** Ed. Hans Küng. 92pp.
45. (Vol. 5 No. 5) **Profession and Responsibility in Society.** Ed. Franz Bockle. 84pp.
46. (Vol. 6 No. 5) **Fundamental Theology.** Ed. Johannes Baptist Metz. 84pp.
47. (Vol. 7 No. 5) **Sacralization in the History of the Church.** Ed. Roger Aubert. 80pp.
48. (Vol. 8 No. 5) **The Dynamism of Canon Law.** Ed. Neophytos Edelby and Teodoro Jimenez Urresti. 92pp.
49. (Vol. 9 No. 5) **An Anxious Society Looks to the Gospel.** Ed. Christian Duquoc. 80pp.
50. (Vol. 10 No. 5) **The Presence and Absence of God.** Ed. Pierre Benoit and Roland Murphy. 88pp.
51. (Vol. 1 No. 6) **Tension between Church and Faith.** Ed. Edward Schillebeeckx. 160pp.
52. (Vol. 2 No. 6) **Prayer and Community.** Ed. Herman Schmidt. 156pp.
53. (Vol. 3 No. 6) **Catechetics for the Future.** Ed. Alois Müller. 168pp.
54. (Vol. 4 No. 6) **Post-Ecumenical Christianity.** Ed. Hans Küng. 168pp.
55. (Vol. 5 No. 6) **The Future of Marriage as Institution.** Ed. Franz Bockle. 180pp.
56. (Vol. 6 No. 6) **Moral Evil Under Challenge.** Ed. Johannes Baptist Metz. 160pp.
57. (Vol. 7 No. 6) **Church History at a Turning Point.** Ed. Roger Aubert. 160pp.
58. (Vol. 8 No. 6) **Structures of the Church's Presence in the World of Today.** Ed. Teodoro Jimenez Urresti. 160pp.
59. (Vol. 9 No. 6) **Hope.** Ed. Christian Duquoc. 160pp.
60. (Vol. 10 No. 6) **Immortality and Resurrection.** Ed. Pierre Benoit and Roland Murphy. 160pp.

61. (Vol. 1 No. 7) **The Sacramental Administration of Reconciliation.** Ed. Edward Schillebeeckx. 160pp.
62. (Vol. 2 No. 7) **Worship of Christian Man Today.** Ed. Herman Schmidt. 156pp.
63. (Vol. 3 No. 7) **Democratization of the Church.** Ed. Alois Müller. 160pp.
64. (Vol. 4 No. 7) **The Petrine Ministry in the Church.** Ed. Hans Küng. 160pp.
65. (Vol. 5 No. 7) **The Manipulation of Man.** Ed. Franz Bockle. 144pp.
66. (Vol. 6 No. 7) **Fundamental Theology in the Church.** Ed. Johannes Baptist Metz. 156pp.
67. (Vol. 7 No. 7) **The Self-Understanding of the Church.** Ed. Roger Aubert. 144pp.
68. (Vol. 8 No. 7) **Contestation in the Church.** Ed. Teodoro Jimenez Urresti. 152pp.
69. (Vol. 9 No. 7) **Spirituality, Public or Private?** Ed. Christian Duquoc. 156pp.
70. (Vol. 10 No. 7) **Theology, Exegesis and Proclamation.** Ed. Roland Murphy. 144pp.
71. (Vol. 1 No. 8) **The Bishop and the Unity of the Church.** Ed. Edward Schillebeeckx. 156pp.
72. (Vol. 2 No. 8) **Liturgy and the Ministry.** Ed. Herman Schmidt. 160pp.
73. (Vol. 3 No. 8) **Reform of the Church.** Ed. Alois Müller and Norbert Greinacher. 152pp.
74. (Vol. 4 No. 8) **Mutual Recognition of Ecclesial Ministries?** Ed. Hans Küng and Walter Kasper. 152pp.
75. (Vol. 5 No. 8) **Man in a New Society.** Ed. Franz Bockle. 160pp.
76. (Vol. 6 No. 8) **The God Question.** Ed. Johannes Baptist Metz. 156pp.
77. (Vol. 7 No. 8) **Election-Consensus-Reception.** Ed. Giuseppe Alberigo and Anton Weiler. 156pp.
78. (Vol. 8 No. 8) **Celibacy of the Catholic Priest.** Ed. William Bassett and Peter Huizing. 160pp.
79. (Vol. 9 No. 8) **Prayer.** Ed. Christian Duquoc and Claude Geffré. 126pp.
80. (Vol. 10 No. 8) **Ministries in the Church.** Ed. Bas van Iersel and Roland Murphy. 152pp.
81. **The Persistence of Religion.** Ed. Andrew Greeley and Gregory Baum. 0 8164 2537 X 168pp.
82. **Liturgical Experience of Faith.** Ed. Herman Schmidt and David Power. 0 8164 2538 8 144pp.
83. **Truth and Certainty.** Ed. Edward Schillebeeckx and Bas van Iersel. 0 8164 2539 6 144pp.
84. **Political Commitment and Christian Community.** Ed. Alois Müller and Norbert Greinacher. 0 8164 2540 X 156pp.
85. **The Crisis of Religious Language.** Ed. Johannes Baptist Metz and Jean-Pierre Jossua. 0 8164 2541 8 144pp.
86. **Humanism and Christianity.** Ed. Claude Geffré. 0 8164 2542 6 144pp.
87. **The Future of Christian Marriage.** Ed. William Bassett and Peter Huizing. 0 8164 2575 2.

88. **Polarization in the Church.** Ed. Hans Küng and Walter Kasper. 0 8164 2572 8 156pp.
89. **Spiritual Revivals.** Ed. Christian Duquoc and Casiano Floristán. 0 8164 2573 6 156pp.
90. **Power and the Word of God.** Ed. Franz Bockle and Jacques Marie Pohier. 0 8164 2574 4 156pp.
91. **The Church as Institution.** Ed. Gregory Baum and Andrew Greeley. 0 8164 2575 2 168pp.
92. **Politics and Liturgy.** Ed. Herman Schmidt and David Power. 0 8164 2576 0 156pp.
93. **Jesus Christ and Human Freedom.** Ed. Edward Schillebeeckx and Bas van Iersel. 0 8164 2577 9 168pp.
94. **The Experience of Dying.** Ed. Norbert Greinacher and Alois Müller. 0 8164 2578 7 156pp.
95. **Theology of Joy.** Ed. Johannes Baptist Metz and Jean-Pierre Jossua. 0 8164 2579 5 164pp.
96. **The Mystical and Political Dimension of the Christian Faith.** Ed. Claude Geffré and Gustavo Guttierez. 0 8164 2580 9 168pp.
97. **The Future of the Religious Life.** Ed. Peter Huizing and William Bassett. 0 8164 2094 7 96pp.
98. **Christians and Jews.** Ed. Hans Küng and Walter Kasper. 0 8164 2095 5 96pp.
99. **Experience of the Spirit.** Ed. Peter Huizing and William Bassett. 0 8164 2096 3 144pp.
100. **Sexuality in Contemporary Catholicism.** Ed. Franz Bockle and Jacques Marie Pohier. 0 8164 2097 1 126pp.
101. **Ethnicity.** Ed. Andrew Greeley and Gregory Baum. 0 8164 2145 5 120pp.
102. **Liturgy and Cultural Religious Traditions.** Ed. Herman Schmidt and David Power. 0 8164 2146 2 120pp.
103. **A Personal God?** Ed. Edward Schillebeeckx and Bas van Iersel. 0 8164 2149 8 142pp.
104. **The Poor and the Church.** Ed. Norbert Greinacher and Alois Müller. 0 8164 2147 1 128pp.
105. **Christianity and Socialism.** Ed. Johannes Baptist Metz and Jean-Pierre Jossua. 0 8164 2148 X 144pp.
106. **The Churches of Africa: Future Prospects.** Ed. Claude Geffré and Bertrand Luneau. 0 8164 2150 1 128pp.
107. **Judgement in the Church.** Ed. William Bassett and Peter Huizing. 0 8164 2166 8 128pp.
108. **Why Did God Make Me?** Ed. Hans Küng and Jürgen Moltmann. 0 8164 2167 6 112pp.
109. **Charisms in the Church.** Ed. Christian Duquoc and Casiano Floristán. 0 8164 2168 4 128pp.
110. **Moral Formation and Christianity.** Ed. Franz Bockle and Jacques Marie Pohier. 0 8164 2169 2 120pp.
111. **Communication in the Church.** Ed. Gregory Baum and Andrew Greeley. 0 8164 2170 6 126pp.

112. **Liturgy and Human Passage.** Ed. David Power and Luis Maldonado. 0 8164 2608 2 136pp.
113. **Revelation and Experience.** Ed. Edward Schillebeeckx and Bas van Iersel. 0 8164 2609 0 134pp.
114. **Evangelization in the World Today.** Ed. Norbert Greinacher and Alois Müller. 0 8164 2610 4 136pp.
115. **Doing Theology in New Places.** Ed. Jean-Pierre Jossua and Johannes Baptist Metz. 0 8164 2611 2 120pp.
116. **Buddhism and Christianity.** Ed. Claude Geffré and Mariasusai Dhavamony. 0 8164 2612 0 136pp.
117. **The Finances of the Church.** Ed. William Bassett and Peter Huizing. 0 8164 2197 8 160pp.
118. **An Ecumenical Confession of Faith?** Ed. Hans Küng and Jürgen Moltmann. 0 8164 2198 6 136pp.
119. **Discernment of the Spirit and of Spirits.** Ed. Casiano Floristán and Christian Duquoc. 0 8164 2199 4 136pp.
120. **The Death Penalty and Torture.** Ed. Franz Bockle and Jacques Marie Pohier. 0 8164 2200 1 136pp.
121. **The Family in Crisis or in Transition.** Ed. Andrew Greeley. 0 567 30001 3 128pp.
122. **Structures of Initiation in Crisis.** Ed. Luis Maldonado and David Power. 0 567 30002 1 128pp.
123. **Heaven.** Ed. Bas van Iersel and Edward Schillebeeckx. 0 567 30003 X 120pp.
124. **The Church and the Rights of Man.** Ed. Alois Müller and Norbert Greinacher. 0 567 30004 8 140pp.
125. **Christianity and the Bourgeoisie.** Ed. Johannes Baptist Metz. 0 567 30005 6 144pp.
126. **China as a Challenge to the Church.** Ed. Claude Geffré and Joseph Spae. 0 567 30006 4 136pp.
127. **The Roman Curia and the Communion of Churches.** Ed. Peter Huizing and Knut Walf. 0 567 30007 2 144pp.
128. **Conflicts about the Holy Spirit.** Ed. Hans Küng and Jürgen Moltmann. 0 567 30008 0 144pp.
129. **Models of Holiness.** Ed. Christian Duquoc and Casiano Floristán. 0 567 30009 9 128pp.
130. **The Dignity of the Despised of the Earth.** Ed. Jacques Marie Pohier and Dietmar Mieth. 0 567 30010 2 144pp.
131. **Work and Religion.** Ed. Gregory Baum. 0 567 30011 0 148pp.
132. **Symbol and Art in Worship.** Ed. Luis Maldonado and David Power. 0 567 30012 9 136pp.
133. **Right of the Community to a Priest.** Ed. Edward Schillebeeckx and Johannes Baptist Metz. 0 567 30013 7 148pp.
134. **Women in a Men's Church.** Ed. Virgil Elizondo and Norbert Greinacher. 0 567 30014 5 144pp.
135. **True and False Universality of Christianity.** Ed. Claude Geffré and Jean-Pierre Jossua. 0 567 30015 3 138pp.

136. **What is Religion? An Inquiry for Christian Theology.** Ed. Mircea Eliade and David Tracy. 0 567 30016 1 98pp.
137. **Electing our Own Bishops.** Ed. Peter Huizing and Knut Walf. 0 567 30017 X 112pp.
138. **Conflicting Ways of Interpreting the Bible.** Ed. Hans Küng and Jürgen Moltmann. 0 567 30018 8 112pp.
139. **Christian Obedience.** Ed. Casiano Floristán and Christian Duquoc. 0 567 30019 6 96pp.
140. **Christian Ethics and Economics: the North-South Conflict.** Ed. Dietmar Mieth and Jacques Marie Pohier. 0 567 30020 X 128pp.
141. **Neo-Conservatism: Social and Religious Phenomenon.** Ed. Gregory Baum and John Coleman. 0 567 30021 8.
142. **The Times of Celebration.** Ed. David Power and Mary Collins. 0 567 30022 6.
143. **God as Father.** Ed. Edward Schillebeeckx and Johannes Baptist Metz. 0 567 30023 4.
144. **Tensions Between the Churches of the First World and the Third World.** Ed. Virgil Elizondo and Norbert Greinacher. 0 567 30024 2.
145. **Nietzsche and Christianity.** Ed. Claude Geffré and Jean-Pierre Jossua. 0 567 30025 0.
146. **Where Does the Church Stand?** Ed. Giuseppe Alberigo. 0 567 30026 9.
147. **The Revised Code of Canon Law: a Missed Opportunity?** Ed. Peter Huizing and Knut Walf. 0 567 30027 7.
148. **Who Has the Say in the Church?** Ed. Hans Küng and Jürgen Moltmann. 0 567 30028 5.
149. **Francis of Assisi Today.** Ed. Casiano Floristán and Christian Duquoc. 0 567 30029 3.
150. **Christian Ethics: Uniformity, Universality, Pluralism.** Ed. Jacques Pohier and Dietmar Mieth. 0 567 30030 7.
151. **The Church and Racism.** Ed. Gregory Baum and John Coleman. 0 567 30031 5.
152. **Can we always celebrate the Eucharist?** Ed. Mary Collins and David Power. 0 567 30032 3.
153. **Jesus, Son of God?** Ed. Edward Schillebeeckx and Johannes-Baptist Metz. 0 567 30033 1.
154. **Religion and Churches in Eastern Europe.** Ed. Virgil ELizondo and Norbert Greinacher. 0 567 30034 X.
155. **'The Human', Criterion of Christian Existence?** Ed. Claude Geffré and Jean-Pierre Jossua. 0 567 30035 8.
156. **The Challenge of Psychology to Faith.** Ed. Steven Kepnes (Guest Editor) and David Tracy. 0 567 30036 6.
157. **May Church Ministers be Politicians?** Ed. Peter Huizing and Knut Walf. 0 567 30037 4.
158. **The Right to Dissent.** Ed. Hans Küng and Jürgen Moltmann. 0 567 30038 2.

CONCILIUM

159. **Learning to pray.** Ed. Casiano Floristán and Christian Duquoc. 0 567 30039 0.
160. **Unemployment and the Right to Work.** Ed. Dietmar Mieth and Jacques Pohier. 0 567 30040 4.
161. **New Religious Movements.** Ed. by John Coleman and Gregory Baum.
162. **Liturgy: A Creative Tradition.** Ed. by Mary Collins and David Power.
163. **Martyrdom Today.** Ed. by Johannes-Baptist Metz and Edward Schillebeeckx.
164. **Church and Peace.** Ed. by Virgil Elizondo and Norbert Greinacher.
165. **Indifference to Religion.** Ed. by Claude Geffré and Jean-Pierre Jossua.
166. **Theology and Cosmology.** Ed. by David Tracy and Nicholas Lash.
167. **The Ecumenical Council and the Church Constitution.** Ed. by Peter Huizing and Knut Walf.
168. **Mary in the Churches.** Ed. by Hans Küng and Jürgen Moltmann.
169. **Job and the Silence of God.** Ed. by Christian Duquoc and Casiano Floristán.

170. **Twenty Years of Concilium—Retrospect and Prospect.** Ed. by Edward Schillebeeckx, Paul Brand and Anton Weiler.
171. **Different Theologies, Common Responsibility: Babel or Pentecost?** Ed. by C. Geffré, G. Gutierrez, V. Elizondo.
172. **The Ethics of Liberation—The Liberation of Ethics.** Ed. by D. Mieth, J. Pohier.
173. **The Sexual Revolution.** Ed. by G. Baum, J. Coleman.
174. **The Transmission of the Faith to the Next Generation.** Ed. by V. Elizondo, D. Tracy.
175. **The Holocaust as Interruption.** Ed. by E. Fiorenza, D. Tracy.
176. **La Iglesia Popular: Between Fear and Hope.** Ed. by L. Boff, V. Elizondo.
177. **Monotheism.** Ed. by Claude Geffré and Jean Pierre Jossua.
178. **Blessing and Power.** Ed. by David Power and Mary Collins.

179. **Suicide and the Right to Die.** Ed. by Jacques Pohier and Dietmar Mieth.
180. **The Teaching Authority of the Believers.** Ed. by Johannes-Baptist Metz and Edward Schillibeeckx.
181. **Youth Without a Future?** Ed. by John Coleman and Gregory Baum.
182. **Women—Invisible in Church and Theology.** Ed. by Elisabeth Fiorenza and Mary Collins.
183. **Christianity Among World Religions.** Ed. by Hans Küng and Jürgen Moltmann.
184. **Forgiveness.** Ed. by Casiano Floristán and Christian Duquoc.
185. **Canon Law—Church Reality.** Ed. by James Provost and Knut Walf.
186. **Popular Religion.** Ed. by Norbert Greinacher and Norbert Mette.
187. **Option for the Poor! Challenge to the Rich Countries.** Ed. by Leonardo Boff and Virgil Elizondo.
188. **Synod 1985: An Evaluation.** Ed. by Giuseppe Alberigo and James Provost.

CONCILIUM 1987

THE EXODUS
Edited by Bas van Iersel and Anton Weiler 189

THE FATE OF CONFESSION
Edited by Mary Collins and David Power 190

CHANGING VALUES AND VIRTUES
Edited by Dietmar Mieth and
Jacques Pohier 191

ORTHODOXY AND HETERODOXY
Edited by Johannes-Baptist Metz
and Edward Schillebeeckx 192

THE CHURCH AND CHRISTIAN DEMOCRACY
Edited by Gregory Baum and John Coleman 193

WOMEN, WORK AND POVERTY
Edited by Elisabeth Schüssler Fiorenza
and Anne Carr 194

All back issues are still in print: available from bookshops (price £5.45) or direct from the publishers (£5.95/US$9.95/Can$11.75 including postage and packing).

**T & T CLARK LTD, 59 GEORGE STREET
EDINBURGH EH2 2LQ, SCOTLAND**

SUBSCRIBE TO CONCILIUM

'**CONCILIUM** a journal of world standing, is far and away the best.'
The Times

'... it is certainly the most variegated and stimulating school of theology active today. **CONCILIUM** ought to be available to all clergy and layfolk who are anxious to keep abreast of what is going on in the theological workshops of the world today.'
Theology

CONCILIUM is published on the first of every alternate month beginning in February. Over twelve issues (two years), themes are drawn from the following key areas: dogma, liturgy, pastoral theology, ecumenism, moral theology, the sociology of religion, Church history, canon law, spirituality, scripture, Third World theology and Feminist theology (see back cover for details of 1988 titles). As a single issue sells for £5.45 a subscription can mean savings of up to £12.75.

SUBSCRIPTION RATES 1988

	UK	USA	Canada	Other Countries
New Subscribers	£19.95	$39.95	$49.95	£19.95
Regular Subscribers	£27.50	$49.95	$59.95	£27.50
Airmail		$65.00	$79.95	£37.50

All prices include postage and packing. **CONCILIUM** is sent 'accelerated surface post' to the USA and Canada and by surface mail to other destinations.

Cheques payable to T & T Clark. Personal cheques in $ currency acceptable. Credit card payments by *Access*, *Mastercard* and *Visa*.

'A bold and confident venture in contemporary theology. All the best new theologians are contributing to this collective summa'.
Commonweal

Send your order direct to the Publishers

T & T CLARK LTD

59 GEORGE STREET
EDINBURGH
EH2 2LQ
SCOTLAND

Publishers   *since 1821*